Employment law for
line managers

Produced and published by:

Watershed Europe
33 St James's Square
London
SW1Y 4JS

ISBN 978 0 9564337 6 3

Copyright © January 2010

Updated 9th edition June 2018

Watershed Europe Limited

Ryecroft, Aviary Road, Worsley, Manchester M28 2WF

Telephone +44 161 703 5611
E-mail: info@watershedhr.com

Printed in the United Kingdom using paper produced from sustainable sources.
Design, typesetting and production – CQ2 Design and Digital www.cq2.co.uk

Employment law for line managers – a new beginning

Collinson Grant has been advising human resources (HR) and line managers on the practical implications and application of employment law for nearly 50 years. Our clients include many commercial organisations throughout the UK.

Collinson Grant also works with clients to restructure, merge acquisitions, cut costs, restore profitability, introduce lean operations, streamline supply chains and manage people better. Our consultancy skills and diverse experience help us to achieve successful results in demanding situations.

More and more clients are accessing our skilled employment law and HR practitioners. We want to continue that growth, which requires a clearer positioning in the external market for that service that is different from our other consultancy services.

So we are rebranding that part of the business as Watershed to enable a distinction between the two parts of our business   hence the change to the cover of this book! Watershed will consist of the same experienced staff as Collinson Grant today, in the same premises, doing the same things. It will retain the same commitment to excellence and value for money. And rest assured, this book will continue!

We will continue to work seamlessly with the wider Collinson Grant family and remain committed to offering an exceptional service, provided by a first-class team of people, who are accessible, professional, pragmatic and have the technical knowledge equal to any provider in the sector.

Watershed helps to improve the performance of employers throughout the United Kingdom, in continental Europe and further afield. We work in all sectors, helping managers on organisation, process, people and costs.

Our specialists support line and human resources managers in every aspect of managing people, particularly on assignments to do with employment law, managing performance, restructuring and reward.

Our services include:
- HR health checks – testing the efficiency and cost-effectiveness of all HR services
- Tailored support contracts – focusing on compliance and the effective, day-to-day management of people
- Resourcing – recruitment and selection, getting value for money from temporary staff
- Managing substantial change – acquisitions, transfers, outsourcing, restructuring
- Dealing with senior staff – appointments, dismissals, contractual issues
- Rewards – pay benchmarking, job sizing and grading frameworks, gender pay reporting, complex remuneration
- Psychometric assessments – testing for recruitment, development and promotion
- Interim management – experienced HR professionals to fill a short or longer-term gap.

www.watershedhr.com

Contents

1. Introduction and the nature of employment law

1   Introduction and the nature of employment law

Watershed HR has grown out of Collinson Grant's employment and HR business, and is our new brand for our Employment Law services.

Collinson Grant started work in the early 1970s. 'Employment law' only truly became a discrete subject with any critical mass in 1971, when the Industrial Relations Act was passed. So we have grown up with it. The law concerning formal relationships and day-to-day behaviour of employees has been a constant consideration in our work supporting clients. And that means we have seen the shape and content of the subject evolve and we understand how best to work with it. It also goes some way to explaining why, by first publishing The Line Manager's Employment Law as far back as 1978, we wanted to emphasise to managers the relevance of employment law to their day-to-day responsibilities.

The legal aspects of employment are, thankfully, not the most important elements in relationships at work, which are also shaped by custom, responsibility and mutual expectation. Traditionally, the law dealt rather with the exceptional situation in which these normal affiliations and behaviours were disrupted – even today, dialogue and interaction in the workplace rarely turn on the nuances of the latest statute or judicial pronouncement. But things have clearly changed.

The extended scope and influence of employment law

Legislation, often supported by codes of practice, has greatly increased the number of rights and duties associated with employment and has affected what each party expects of the relationship. Consequently, the law has moved from the wings and is now situated nearer the centre of the stage. Workers may challenge managers' decisions, and may apply to the employment tribunal for redress. Of course, notwithstanding at least temporary preservation in 'the Great Repeal' legislation, post-Brexit the ultimate survival or ongoing judicial treatment of those laws derived from European Union membership must be open to speculation. However, overall, most employment rights are here to stay. Meanwhile, the law on the responsibilities of trade unions, their officers and their actions in support of their members' interests often changes under political pressure. The relative importance of the two basic strands, individual and collective, as well as that of particular subjects within them, alters. But it cannot be seriously doubted that the overall significance of employment law has grown.

The direct financial cost of infringing legal standards can be overestimated: perceptions are fuelled by reports in the media of atypical awards of compensation in some high-profile cases. But, even in more commonplace situations, awards can still be high. And the calculation of that particular exposure does not encompass the frequently irrecoverable legal fees, the 'opportunity cost' of managers' lost time, possible damage to employee relations and adverse publicity in the wider community.

Know the law – constraints and opportunities

Line managers must acquire a working knowledge of the basic contours of employment law to avoid elementary errors that might impair their credibility or harm the business. They should be able to recognise when specialist advice is necessary. And they might also conclude that the law's standards can help improve motivation and performance by providing a foundation for better communication, greater consistency and a sense of participation.

This book, the successor to The Line Manager's Employment Law, which ran for 25 editions over 30 years, seeks to continue providing that required understanding. Although still clearly based on its predecessor, it aims to give the law more life. So it adds detail, essential points, tips on practical things to do, and illustrations of common errors or misconceptions. Regardless of when each edition goes to print, there are always legislative changes lined up for the coming few years but not yet in force. So, we use a Change Alert marker to let the reader know what they should be watching or preparing for. To the extent these rely on political pronouncements, they have often been difficult to gauge and present. Summary reportage in the media being what it is, we have always had to be cognisant of the old saying 'Never let the truth get in the way of a good story'.

The text covers the main provisions of employment law in England, Wales and Scotland. In Northern Ireland the substantive law can be different in some aspects, so seek more guidance if you need it. The law described in this book generally covers only people working in the UK. But the House of Lords (before being superseded by the Supreme Court) decided that some of the main statutory protections can also be extended to employees of UK entities working overseas. Again, professional advice should be sought on the specific situation.

Employment law – some introductory concepts

Scope and foundations

Our employment law is made up of legislation (EU Regulations and Directives or UK Acts and Regulations) and decisions of the courts (case law). These two sources establish the rules that regulate the relationship between an employer and an employee. Sometimes the law makes a distinction between an 'employee' and a 'worker'. In either case, the relationship is based on the existence of a contract.

Contracts

There are different types of contract. These are discussed in more detail later. Generally, a contract is based on freely-given agreement. So an employer has the freedom to decide with whom to make a contract and with whom not to. There are some restrictions on this freedom, most of which are in the laws against discrimination. The detailed contents, or 'terms and conditions', of a contract between an employer and employee or worker record the agreed rights and duties, the provisions for terminating the contract and, sometimes, responsibilities (such as confidentiality) after termination.

Minimum rights

Although it is assumed that both parties enter into the contract voluntarily, legislation establishes minimum rights and standards that apply to the relationship. These override even a contract that does not mention them, or says that some or all of them do not apply, or specifies inferior provisions. Most of the standards described in this book are the minimum ones prescribed by legislation. This book is not overlain with statutory references and sources, of which there are many. However, the main pieces of current UK employment legislation, which have all been amended to a greater or lesser extent since their introduction, are:

■ Employment Rights Act 1996
■ Equality Act 2010
■ Trade Union and Labour Relations (Consolidation) Act 1992
■ Transfer of Undertakings (Protection of Employment) Regulations 2006
■ National Minimum Wage Act 1998
■ Working Time Regulations 1998

So, contractual provisions will only be effective if they at least match, or improve on, any overlapping statutory rules. They will be ineffective, and unenforceable, if they attempt to lessen or avoid the statutory provisions. If a subject is not directly regulated by legislation, the parties (although usually the employer) may specify whatever terms they wish, provided that this does not result in an agreement to do something illegal.

How are employment rights and duties enforced?

Statutory rights and duties are, with a few exceptions, enforced through the employment tribunal system. Employment tribunals can also deal with contractual claims, which are not established by legislation, of a certain type and maximum value. Otherwise, contractual claims are heard by the County Court or High Court.

2. Employees – establishing who they are

2 Employees – establishing who they are

Many statutory rights at work are available only to 'employees' who work under a 'contract of employment' (although 'employee shareholders' may be excluded from some of them – see below). Fewer are available to other providers of work or services who operate as independent contractors under a 'contract for services'. For this reason, it can become necessary to determine whether someone is (or was) an employee or some other type of provider of work. This may also be important to determine who should pay income tax and National Insurance contributions.

An employee or not?

The main questions to be considered are:

- Who has control over how the work is done?
- To what extent is the person integrated into the structure of the organisation? For example, is he or she subject to the employer's disciplinary procedure?
- Who provides the equipment or materials necessary to do the work?
- Must the work be done personally, or may it be delegated to someone else?
- Is there 'mutuality of obligation' (an obligation on one party to provide work and on the other to do it)?
- How are payments processed and how are they treated for tax and National Insurance?
- Does the person have access to benefits, such as sick pay and pension?
- Are there restrictions on the person's freedom to work for others?

Workers

Some workplace rights are available to 'workers'. A 'worker' is defined more widely than an employee. The term includes people who are technically self-employed but who are nevertheless obliged to do work personally. This could include an independent contractor.

Someone who is neither a worker nor an employee is not covered by statutory employment rights. Such people are regarded as being 'in business on their own account'. The main distinction between workers and people in business on their own account is that workers (like employees) have an obligation of personal performance, that is, to do the work themselves.

Contractual position

Casual workers, who include intermittent, 'bank' and seasonal staff, often operate under short-term contracts of employment, each lasting for the brief period they are engaged to work. Formally, there is considered to be no ongoing legal commitment between the parties to work together again.

However, if, historically, they have been engaged to work with sufficient frequency, they may also be able to argue that their overall relationship with the work provider, spanning all the separate, short-term periods of work, is an 'umbrella' contract of employment. This would be on the grounds that the regular provision of work and agreement to do it create a 'mutuality of obligation' between the two parties (see above). If this is the case, continuous service (important for some statutory rights) can be calculated to include even the weeks that fell between the discrete periods of actual work.

Zero-hours workers (ZHWs)

One aspect of casual working – the application of exclusivity clauses to ZHWs - is subject to specific regulation by employment legislation.

A ZHW is one who works under a zero-hours contract (ZHC) or a non-contractual zero-hours arrangement (ZHA).

A ZHC is one under which:

■ the undertaking [by a worker] to do or perform work or services is an undertaking to do so conditionally on the employer making work or services available to the worker; and
■ there is no certainty that any such work or services will be made available to the worker.

A ZHA is one under which an employer and an individual agree terms on which the latter will do work made available by the former but there are no obligations to provide or accept work.

Within a ZHC or ZHA, any clause that seeks to tie the ZHW to the employer by prohibiting work for another employer, either absolutely or without the former's consent – an exclusivity clause – is unenforceable.

Note: There is provision for this protection to be extended by Regulations to encompass working relationships that, although not literal ZHCs, do not guarantee a specified minimum level of pay.

Conflicting terms and practice

Even if a contract contains some terms that are associated only with a certain status (generally, 'self-employment'), a court or tribunal can look behind it to examine the way the overall relationship actually operates, or did operate. If that analysis points to another status (generally, 'employment'), the court or tribunal can ignore the conflicting words of the contract and find that an individual is or was a worker or, even, an employee, with corresponding access to statutory protections. This has become particularly pertinent with the working patterns and arrangements associated with the 'gig' economy.

Employee shareholders

Under an agreement to take shares in the employer's business worth £2,000 or more (for agreements made before December 2016, up to £2,000 being exempt from income tax and up to £100,000 being exempt from Capital Gains Tax), an employee can choose to forfeit the rights to:

- give only eight weeks' notice of early return from maternity or adoption leave (see Chapter 5), instead having to give 16 weeks
- request flexible working (see Chapter 5)
- request study or training (see Chapter 7)
- claim unfair dismissal (see Chapter 10) unless the dismissal contravenes the equality laws (see Chapter 8) or is for an 'automatically unfair' reason (see Chapter 10)
- receive a statutory redundancy payment (see Chapter 11).

Employee shareholder contracts can:

- be offered to existing employees (as an alternative to their current arrangements) but not imposed upon them;
- be the only arrangement offered to new recruits (who will not be automatically disqualified from Jobseeker's Allowance for failing to accept the arrangement).

In either case, an agreement for a person to become an employee shareholder will be ineffective unless, beforehand, the person:

- first receives from the employer a written statement of the employment rights affected by shareholder status and the nature of and rights associated with the shares offered; and
- then receives advice from a lawyer or other relevant independent adviser (whose reasonable costs must be met by the employer, regardless of whether an employee shareholder agreement is concluded) at least seven days before the agreement.

Change alert: while, despite the removal of tax reliefs for employee shareholder agreements made from December 2016 onwards, new agreements are still lawful, the Government has indicated its wish to abolish employee shareholder status altogether, although no steps have yet been taken.

Apprentices

Whether engaged under a traditional contract of apprenticeship or under more recent statutory arrangements – an approved English apprenticeship under an apprenticeship framework, an apprenticeship agreement in Wales, or a Scottish modern apprenticeship – an apprentice is an 'employee' with access to most of the statutory employment protections (an exception is discrimination against fixed-term employees – see Chapter 8).

However, a traditional contract of apprenticeship, which has its primary focus on training and is for a fixed-term without provision for early termination with notice, cannot generally be terminated partway through the term without exposure to an award of damages, which will be enhanced to take account of career opportunities lost through incomplete training. As a result most apprentices are taken on under the statutory apprenticeship arrangements. It is a criminal offence to call a role 'an apprenticeship' unless it meets the legal requirements for one.

The apprenticeship levy was introduced by section 98 to 121 of the Finance Act 2016. It is payable with effect from 6th April 2017 by employers through PAYE alongside income tax and NICs if the pay bill exceeds £3m in the previous year. HMRC has published an Apprenticeship Levy Manual that can be found on the gov.uk website.

Levy-paying employers with employees located in England, will be able to set up a Digital Apprenticeship Service account that will contain funds they can spend on apprenticeship training and assessment costs in England.

If the employer is levy-paying, with operations based wholly or partly in Scotland, Wales or Northern Ireland, they will need to engage with the relevant authorities for funding apprenticeships located there as apprenticeships are a devolved policy.

Regulation of employment businesses

An 'employment business' (often known as an employment agency) may directly employ people seeking work under a contract of employment and supply them temporarily to work for, and be controlled by, a hiring organisation. Or the person supplied by the agency may work under a contract for services and so not be regarded as an employee of the agency. The agency must confirm, in writing, to both the work seeker and the hirer whether the worker is its employee or is working under a contract for services.

An employment relationship directly with the hirer?

Courts or tribunals have been known to decide that someone hired out by an employment business had, through a lengthy relationship and 'mutuality of obligation', an implied contract of employment with the hirer. However, that approach is now favoured only in very exceptional circumstances.

Parity of terms

'Agency' workers hired out for an assignment that is not open-ended (or 'permanent') who have completed a 12-week qualifying period have the right to the same pay and basic terms and conditions (such as hours, rest breaks/periods and annual leave) from the employment business/temporary work agency (TWA) as would have applied had they been recruited directly by the hirer.

Note: there is an exemption from the pay element for a TWA that has engaged an agency worker under a 'permanent' contract of employment that provides for payment between assignments at a rate that is at least 50% of that for assignments and at least equivalent to the national minimum wage' (see Chapter 4). This is sometimes known as 'the Swedish derogation'.

The agency worker must accrue the 12-week qualifying period with a single hirer (but not necessarily through a single TWA) and in the same job or substantively similar ones, on one or more 'assignments'. A break of less than six weeks within an assignment or between assignments will not break continuity. Any change in a job that does occur will not break continuity unless the TWA has confirmed it in writing to the agency worker.

Although the central responsibility and liability for any necessary improvement in the agency worker's terms lie largely with the TWA, the hirer also has direct obligations:

- to give hired agency workers, immediately on commencement, the same access to 'facilities' (such as canteen and childcare) as its own employees;
- to notify the TWA about any changes in the agency worker's role;
- to provide the TWA with information about the pay and terms and conditions applicable if the agency worker had been directly recruited; and
- if the TWA has failed to pass that information on to an agency worker, to provide the agency worker directly with that information within 28 days.

Enforcement, by application to the employment tribunal, is generally against the TWA that has the contract of employment or contract for services with the worker, but, if the hirer has caused or contributed to a breach, may be against it too. The tribunal can award loss of earnings or, for denial of facilities, other appropriate compensation.

A tribunal also has the power to deem the 12-week qualifying period satisfied (and to make an award of up to £5,000) if it considers that actual satisfaction was intentionally defeated by an artificial 'structure of assignments'.

Use of temporary labour during industrial action

Legislation prohibits an employment business from knowingly supplying a worker (a) to do the work of one of the hirer's employees if that employee is participating in official industrial action, or (b) to do the job of another employee who has been transferred by the hirer to cover for the employee who is on strike or taking other industrial action.

Change alert: On 7 February 2018 the Government published its wide-ranging response to the Taylor Review of Modern Working Practices. The response sets out a number of proposals specifically affecting agency workers, including day-one rights for all workers. The Government has since launched a further consultation on some of the recommendations, including removal of the Swedish derogation.

3. The contract

3   The contract

There are three main types of statutory restriction:

Discrimination

Discrimination because of any of the 'protected characteristics' featured in the equality legislation (see Chapter 8) is unlawful.

Membership of a trade union

It is unlawful to refuse employment on grounds that a person:

- is, or is not, a member of a trade union
- will not agree to become, to cease to be, to remain or to refuse to be a member of a trade union
- will not agree to make payments or have deductions made from pay for not being a member of a trade union
- features on a prohibited 'blacklist' (see below).

Compensation for a successful complaint to an employment tribunal can be up to £83,682.

Note: legislation prohibits the making, use, sale or supply of 'blacklists' of trade unionists. Infringements are subject to an action for breach of statutory duty. The court can issue orders to restrain or prevent a party from breach and can award damages (which may cover injury to feelings). Separately, proceedings in the employment tribunal are available for alleged refusals to employ (see above) and for discrimination and dismissal to do with reliance on information on a 'blacklist'.

Employment of illegal migrants

For employment that started on or before 28th February 2008, it is a criminal offence to employ a migrant aged 16 or over who does not have permission to work in the UK. The offence carries a fine of up to £5,000.

For employment that started after 28th February 2008, there are two types of offence:

■ **negligently employing an illegal migrant.** This carries a 'civil penalty' of up to £20,000. The employer has a possible defence if it conducted a pre-employment check of one or more acceptable documents (the legislation provides a list of these) that prove the person's right to work in the UK, either indefinitely or for a limited period. However, if it is for a limited period, any defence derived from the pre-employment check will lapse after 12 months, unless further checks have been made.

If TUPE (see Chapter 9) applies, the incoming employer has 60 days to comply with the checking requirements for this offence.

■ **knowingly employing an illegal migrant.** This includes where they knew or 'had reasonable cause to believe' the employee did not have the right to work. Conviction following indictment for this criminal offence carries a prison term of up to two years and/or an unlimited fine.

In both cases it is not only the employing company that faces prosecution. Its directors, managers and other senior officers can also be prosecuted if the offence is committed with their consent or collusion, or because of their neglect.

It is a defence to show that, before recruitment, the employee produced a document specified in the legislation that appeared to refer to him or her and the employer kept it or took a copy of it. This defence applies even if the document turns out to be fraudulent, unless the employer knew that it would be illegal to employ the person.

Slavery and Human Trafficking Statement

Commercial organisations (those supplying goods or services, even if their aims or functions are primarily charitable, educational or public) with a demonstrable business presence in the UK and a minimum annual turnover of £36 million (including that of any subsidiaries, wherever they conduct business) are required, for each financial year ending on or after 31st March 2016, to produce and publish an annual Slavery and Human Trafficking Statement.

The statement must include either a description of steps taken during the year to ensure slavery and human trafficking is not taking place in any part of its own business or supply chain or a declaration that no such steps have been taken.

It must be approved by the organisation's directors, be signed by one and published on the organisation's website (with a clear link from the homepage).

The duty is enforceable by civil proceedings brought by the Secretary of State for Home Affairs.

The creation of a contract and its consequences

A contract of employment (and a contract for services) is formed as soon as a candidate accepts an offer of employment from an employer. However, a candidate's acceptance will have no effect if the employer has communicated withdrawal of the offer before that acceptance is received.

It is also legitimate for an offer to make any agreement on subsequent acceptance conditional on the prospective employer's receipt of satisfactory references, criminal record checks and medical reports (but do note that enquiries about a candidate's health before an offer or shortlisting could be the subject of enforcement action – see Chapter 8). If those conditions are not satisfied, the contract did not, technically, ever come into being and employment can be terminated.

Once a contract is formed, the employee (or worker) and the employer are bound by its terms. A basic contract will be created even before the work has started or payment has been made for it. This contract could be terminated before the person starts work. If, as sometimes happens, an employer terminates the contract without notice (often saying, incorrectly, that 'the offer is withdrawn'), the amount of damages is normally equivalent to pay for the contractual period of notice or, if none is specified, 'reasonable notice'.

Basic types of contract

A contract can be either:

- 'open-ended', of indefinite duration (sometimes called 'permanent') but capable of being ended with a period of notice; or
- for a limited term (the parties agree at the outset that it will expire on a given date or on the completion of a particular task or occurrence of a specified event), but often capable of being ended sooner with a period of notice.

Common misconception (1)

'....the expiry of a limited-term contract cannot have any legal consequences'

It can, even though the parties agreed at the outset that it would come to an end. Expiry without renewal amounts to a dismissal (see Chapter 10). And, although the employer generally has a head start in defending any allegation of unfair dismissal (the expiry was agreed at the outset and is often because there is no more work), there can be problems.

Difficulties can arise if a particular employee was not offered continuation in the post under another contract (and someone else was recruited) because of some unacceptable reason. Or, it could be that, although the particular post lapsed with the expiry of the contract, there was alternative employment that was not properly considered.

In any event, there is always the need for an employer to notify (or remind) the employee of the prospect that employment will end and to apply an appropriate pre-termination procedure.

Recording terms

To reduce the likelihood of, and scope for, misunderstanding or dispute, a written contract or a written record of the main provisions is desirable.

The written statement of employment particulars

In any event, it is a statutory requirement that an employee must be provided with this statement within two months of starting work. The statement is not, strictly, the contract of employment – it is merely evidence of the main terms of the contract. However, employers often include the subjects required by law (see the list below) in a broader, formal contract of employment, which also contains provisions on other matters (such as company cars, other benefits, and restrictions on post-termination activities).

What the statement of employment particulars must contain:

1 date(s) when employment and continuous employment began
2 scale or rate of remuneration or method of its calculation
3 intervals at which remuneration is paid
4 hours of work
5 holiday entitlement and arrangements
6 place of work or, if various places of work are contemplated, an indication of that and the employer's address
7 job title or brief description of the work
8 arrangements for sickness and pension
9 disciplinary rules and procedure, and procedures for dismissal
10 grievance procedure
11 particulars of any collective agreements directly affecting terms and conditions or, if none, a statement to that effect
12 entitlement to notice
13 expiry date of a fixed-term contract or the expected duration of any other temporary contract
14 if the employee is required to work outside the UK for more than one month, the duration of that period, any additional remuneration or benefits and any terms and conditions about return to the UK.

Information can be given in instalments and by reference

Employment particulars (1) – (14) may be given in instalments, as long as the employee is provided with all the information within two months of starting.

Points (1) to (7) must, however, be contained in a single document. This is known as the 'principal statement'. Items (8) to (14) may also be in that document, or in a subsequent statement.

For items (8) to (11), it is permitted to make reference to other documents, specifying where those other documents may be found. For item (12), it is permitted to make reference to legislation or a collective agreement with a trade union.

If no information is to be provided under any heading, this must be stated.

If there are changes to the required content

Any change to the required content of the statement must be notified to the employee personally, in writing, within one month of the change.

This does not, in itself, mean that the employer has the legal right to change contractual terms without the employee's consent – it simply imposes an obligation on the employer to record a change that has occurred.

The employee's right to consult the employment tribunal

An employee can apply to the employment tribunal to determine employment particulars.

In addition, if an employee succeeds in a claim to the tribunal about a separate right (such as unfair dismissal) and the tribunal finds that the employer has not complied with the duty to provide particulars, it can award between two and four weeks' pay (at a maximum of £508) per week) to the (ex-)employee.

There are four main types of contractual term:

- Express – they have been stated orally and/or recorded in writing. They have been expressly agreed between the parties and can only be overridden by legislation. An express term will be void if it attempts to deprive someone of statutory rights.
- Implied – derived from case law, where necessary, to plug gaps left by the express terms and make sense of the employment relationship.
- Incorporated – expressly or by implication, from other sources such as a collective agreement, works rules or company handbook. But terminology can be important. In one case, the (unsuccessful) claimant's statement of employment terms said the 'basic terms and conditions of [your] employment are in accordance with and subject to the provisions' of the collective agreement. The collective agreement included a redundancy procedure. But the court decided it was not incorporated. The meaning of the words used was that 'the basic terms and conditions' were those in the collective agreement. The basic terms were only those required by the statutory principal statement of employment particulars (see above) – so the redundancy procedure was not contractual.
- Statutory – derived from provisions of statutes (such as an 'equality clause' inserted by the law on equal pay – see Chapter 4).

Implied terms exist in every contract. They are not shown in the statement of particulars or a written contract of employment, yet they still place obligations on the employer, the employee, or both. Implied terms are those that are:

■ regarded as integral to a personal relationship, such as mutual trust and confidence, or the exercise of reasonable care and skill;
■ considered so obvious to the effective working of the relationship, or a particular aspect of it, that the parties would have included them had they been asked or thought about it; or
■ based on 'custom and practice' or the conduct of the parties.

The relationship between implied terms and express termss

An implied term in a contract cannot override an express (explicitly stated) term that contradicts it on the same subject (an aspect of pay for example, such as overtime rates). However, implied terms are often about standards of conduct. For example, say a contract contains the express right to put the employee on 'other duties'. It is possible for that right to be exercised in such a harsh or unreasonable way that it amounts to a breach of an implied term (particularly that of trust and confidence).

The importance of trust and confidence

The implied obligation of trust and confidence is so central to employment that any breach of it entitles the injured party to treat the contract as not just breached but also ended. An injured employer will be able to dismiss without notice (generally, only provided that a proper investigation takes place and a satisfactory procedure is followed – see Chapter 10). A wronged employee will be able to resign and to be treated as 'constructively' dismissed (see Chapter 10).

'That's it, I've had enough'

How does one decide whether a party has terminated a contract?

In many cases, there will be no doubt. The intention of the employer or employee will be quite clear from the natural meaning of the words used in a letter or a conversation. And subsequent behaviour will generally confirm the fact.

But there are situations in which the context and significance of words and/or actions have to be considered more carefully, either by the party to whom they are addressed or by the employment tribunal. Ambiguity of wordings and contradictory messages are often the problem. On other occasions, even combinations of words with a superficially clear meaning merit further evaluation.

For example, in a heated dispute, an employee says on leaving, 'That's it, I've had enough'. If the employer takes that utterance literally and proceeds to treat the employee as having resigned, there may be difficulty.

Many of the immediate, post-departure measures that an employer takes (P45, collection of company property, denial of access to the computer system) are the same as those that are taken when there is a dismissal. This means that an overly hasty, unverified or unforgiving response to words spoken by an employee in the heat of the moment can end up as amounting to exclusion by the employer and, effectively, a dismissal.

See Chapter 10 for more information about the termination of contracts.

4. Statutory employment rights – pay, hours and holidays

4 Statutory employment rights – pay, hours and holidays

National minimum wage (including national living wage)

A worker (not just an employee) has the right to receive the national minimum wage (NMW) unless he or she is:

- a student or trainee on work placement
- a voluntary worker
- living in the employer's home, working as part of the family and not paying for subsistence (such as an au pair).

The hourly rates of the NMW and the national living wage (NLW) are reviewed every April and are set as:

	From April 2017	From April 2018
Aged 25 or over (the NLW)	£7.50	£7.83
Aged 21-24	£7.05	£7.38
Aged 18-20 and those aged 21 or over who are in the first six months of a job under an accredited training scheme	£5.60	£5.90
Aged 16-17	£4.05	£4.20
Apprentice aged under 19 or in the first year of apprenticeship	£3.50	£3.70

How is the hourly rate calculated?

To calculate the hourly rate (to determine compliance with the NMW), an employee's total gross pay is divided by the number of hours worked during the 'pay reference period'.

Gross pay includes commission, bonuses, and gratuities paid through the payroll. It excludes payment for overtime, shift premiums, allowances for unsocial hours, London weighting, stand-by payments, and gratuities received directly from customers.

The pay reference period (PRP) is one month, unless the worker is paid weekly or daily, in which case it is the shorter period. If the work done in one PRP is not actually paid until the next PRP (for example, because payment is made monthly in arrears), the pay can be attributed to the earlier PRP to calculate the hourly rate.

The method for calculating the hourly rate depends on the type of work involved:

- **time work** (payment by the number of hours 'worked', wherever the location). Admissible hours include those on business travel during normal working time and on stand-by or on-call near the workplace (but not at home) but exclude rest-breaks or absences
- **salaried work** (payment in equal instalments through the year for a set minimum number of hours). Admissible hours are the same as for time work, except that absences attracting normal pay and rest breaks that form part of basic hours are counted
- **output work** (payment according to the amount of work done, for example the number of items produced or sales made, unless this is classified as time work). Payment must be either for hours worked on business travel plus every hour of actual work, or according to a 'fair piece rate'. A fair piece rate is set at 1.2 times the time taken by an average worker of the employer to earn the NMW. This gives workers who may be below average the opportunity to earn the NMW. The fair piece rate must be notified to the worker in writing
- **unmeasured work** (that is, not 'time work', 'salaried work' or 'output work'). This includes work for which there are no specified hours. Admissible hours are those spent on business travel plus either every hour of actual work or those fixed by a 'daily average agreement'. This is a written agreement made before the start of the pay reference period that it covers, stating the average hours the employee is expected to work each day.

Pay records must be kept for three years

Records of pay and any daily average agreements must be kept for this period. The worker can make a written request to see personal pay records and to copy them. An employer's refusal of a request, or failure to respond to one, can lead an employment tribunal to award the worker a sum equal to 80 times the NMW.

How is the minimum rate enforced?

On investigation, HMRC may issue a Notice of Underpayment requiring the employer both to make good the underpayment and to pay a financial penalty of 200% of the shortfall (subject to a minimum of £100 and maximum of £20,000) for each affected worker. Compliance within 14 days will result in a reduction of the penalty by 50%. HMRC also produces a publicly accessible list of employers that they have found have not complied with the NMW.

In the event of further non-compliance, HMRC can take criminal proceedings against the employer or commence tribunal or court proceedings to secure the arrears on behalf of the affected worker(s).

Workers may themselves enforce an entitlement to the NMW by presenting a claim for an unlawful deduction from wages (see below) to the employment tribunal or by bringing an action for breach of contract in the civil courts.

A worker has the right not to be subjected to a detriment by the employer for relying on entitlements to the NMW. A successful complaint to the employment tribunal that the worker has been victimised for doing so can result in compensation.

Itemised pay statement

Employees have the right to receive an itemised statement that sets out gross earnings, net pay, and fixed and variable deductions. An employee can complain to the employment tribunal if no statement has been provided, or if the statement does not refer to an 'unnotified deduction' (a deduction that the employee has not been told about, even if it is otherwise valid). The tribunal may award compensation up to a maximum of the total unnotified deductions in the 13 weeks before the complaint was made.

Deductions from pay

Deductions from a worker's 'wages' (this covers salary) are unlawful, unless:

- the deduction is allowed by statute (such as National Insurance, tax and court orders)
- the deduction is provided for in the contract, or
- the worker has given written consent for the deduction before the deduction was made.

The same restrictions apply to any requirement or demand for a worker to make payments to the employer from his or her 'wages'. Some types of deduction or payment are excluded from this specific requirement for clear authority, including those to reimburse overpayments (which must, nevertheless, be shown to have been made – otherwise, the employer could be sued in the ordinary courts for the money due).

As well as salary, the expression 'wages' includes holiday pay, bonus, commission and certain statutorily-based payments, including Statutory Sick Pay, Statutory Maternity Pay, Statutory Paternity Pay, Statutory Adoption Pay and Statutory Shared Parental Pay. However, the definition of 'wages' excludes compensatory severance payments.

A 'deduction' occurs when a worker receives less than the amount that is 'properly payable' according to the contract or any other legal obligation or commitment. So, for example, an employer's non-payment of remuneration for time that a worker spent taking industrial action, whether 'official' or not (see Chapter 14) would not be a 'deduction' – because, subject to certain exceptions (such as annual leave or sickness), the worker is not entitled to receive pay for time spent absent from work.

A worker can complain to the employment tribunal about an unlawful deduction from pay or an unlawful payment demanded by the employer. The claim should be presented to the tribunal within three months of the unlawful deduction concerned.

Note: *Where there is a tribunal claim about a linked series of deductions or underpayments of a particular type, some of which occurred more than three months before presentation of the claim, the entire series can be considered by the tribunal provided the last deduction or underpayment in the series occurred in the three months preceding the claim. For claims presented on or after 1st July 2015, however, awards of back pay are limited to two years, except where the claim is for statutorily-based payments (see above).*

If a claim is successful, the employer will be ordered to reimburse the employee and will lose the right to recoup the money in the future. The employer may also be required to compensate the employee for any additional financial loss suffered because of the unlawful deduction or payment.

In retail, deductions for stock deficiencies or cash shortages are, in any event, limited to 10% (gross) of any single instalment of pay (except for the final one, for which no limit applies).

The deduction of trade union subscriptions from pay by the employer ('check-off') requires the employee's written authorisation before the deduction is made. Otherwise, the deduction is recoverable (from the employer) by complaint to the employment tribunal.

Guarantee payment

An employee is entitled to a guarantee payment for any day on which he or she is temporarily laid off. The payment is based on the 'guaranteed hourly rate'. This is calculated by dividing 'one week's pay' by the contractual number of weekly hours and multiplying the result by the number of hours of work lost on the day in question. Reviewed annually, from April 2018, the maximum guarantee payment is £28.00 per day.

The entitlement to guarantee payments is, for a normal five-day working week, limited to five days in any rolling three-month period. Payment may be made only if:

- the employee has had at least one month's continuous employment
- the lay-off is not due to a trade dispute
- the employee has not unreasonably refused to do suitable alternative work
- the entitlement has not been exhausted in the previous three months.

An employee can complain to the employment tribunal that a guarantee payment is due. If this is successful, the tribunal may order the employer to pay the amount due.

There is a possible exemption from the right to a guarantee payment if a collective agreement already makes provision.

Relationship to the employer's contractual liability

Whatever the employee's contract says about reducing or eliminating pay where there is a shortage of work, the guarantee payment is an employer's unavoidable obligation. But, unless an employee's contract clearly allows for lay-off without pay or for short-time working on reduced pay, the employer will be liable to pay the full contractual daily or weekly rate (which will include the statutory guarantee payment). If the employer fails to pay the full contractual rate, it will be in breach of contract and open to claims for unlawful deduction from wages (see above). If the employee resigns and establishes 'constructive' dismissal, the employer will be open to claims for unfair dismissal and/or a statutory redundancy payment (see Chapters 10 and 11).

Other liability for lay-off or short-time working

There are separate statutory provisions giving an employee the right to claim a statutory redundancy payment after a specified period of short-time working and/or lay-off (see Chapter 11). These use a different definition of 'lay-off', based on a full week without work.

Pay for medical suspension

Employees have a right to pay for up to 26 weeks if specified health and safety regulations require them to be suspended from work. This provision does not cover absence for 'ordinary' sickness or injury.

Conditions for payment and for enforcement are similar to those for a guarantee payment. An employment tribunal is able to award up to 26 weeks' pay to a successful complainant.

Statutory sick pay

Statutory Sick Pay (SSP) is payable for a maximum of 28 weeks in any period of incapacity for work or linked periods of incapacity. A period of incapacity for work is an absence from work because of illness of at least four days, whether or not these are working days.

Exceptions to this include employees:

- on short contracts of service
- with earnings below the lower earnings limit for National Insurance Contributions
- who are sick within 57 days of being paid certain state benefits, such as sickness benefits and maternity allowances
- who have done no work under the contract of service
- involved in a trade dispute
- who have received the maximum SSP
- working abroad, outside the European Union
- in legal custody.

Responsibility for direct payment (as 'incapacity benefit') is transferred to the Department for Work and Pensions (DWP):

- at the beginning of the incapacity if the employee is excluded as above, or
- after the maximum entitlement to SSP, or
- when liability ceases for some other reason, such as when employment ends.

Statutory sick pay (with effect from April 2018)

Normal Weekly Earnings	Weekly SSP
Below £116.00	nil
£113.00 or more	£92.05

The payment rates are reviewed every April, and are increased in line with any rise in the Consumer Prices Index (CPI) to the previous September.

Pension auto-enrolment

From its 'staging date' (between April 2014 and April 2015 for employers with 50-249 workers, between June 2015 and April 2017 for those with fewer than 50 and between May 2017 and February 2018 for new employers set up between April 2012 and September 2017), an employer must automatically enrol each 'eligible jobholder' who is not already a member of a qualifying pension arrangement into a suitable pension scheme.

New employers setting up business from 1 October 2017 onwards, will have an immediate duty to apply automatic auto-enrolment if they pay earnings that attract PAYE deductions.

The employer is required to provide information about auto-enrolment, the pension scheme concerned, and the right to opt-out (see below).

Suitability as an auto-enrolment scheme is assessed by different criteria according to whether the scheme is defined contribution (the employer can generally self-certify), defined benefit or hybrid.

An eligible jobholder is a permanent or temporary employee or an agency worker who is:

■ aged between 22 and state pension age; and
■ earns at least £10,000 per year (for tax year 2017/18) – the 'earnings trigger'.

The employer can postpone enrolment for up to three months.

From 6th April 2018 on enrolment, the minimum contributions are 5% with the employer contributing at least 2% (employee contributions of 3%). Then from 6th April 2019 onwards, the minimum contribution is 8% with the employer contributing at least 3% (employee contributions of 5%). In 2018/19, contributions are calculated on earnings between £6,032 and £46,350.

Those automatically enrolled have the right to opt out, but a jobholder who exercises this right will be automatically re-enrolled every three years.

Non-eligible jobholders can 'opt in' to the automatic enrolment scheme by serving notice on their employer. However, those who earn less than the lower end of the qualifying earnings band (£6,032 in 2018/19) will not be entitled to benefit from any employer's contributions.

Criminal offences (through the Pensions Regulator) attach to recruitment practices or inducements designed to encourage individuals to opt out.

Workers can make a complaint to the employment tribunal if they are subjected to detriment or dismissed for pursuing their rights or benefits (real or perceived) on auto-enrolment.

Equal pay

Scope and conditions

Legislation requires, in certain circumstances (see below), equality in contractual terms and conditions of employment (including rates of pay and pensions) for men and women. The rules described here are one part of the laws to eliminate discrimination because of sex (which, along with other aspects of equality law, are described in Chapter 8).

Contracts of employment are deemed to contain a sex 'equality clause' and occupational pension schemes a 'sex equality rule'. Each secures equal pay/pensions if a female and a male are both employed:

- *'in the same employment'*, that is, in the same 'establishment', or in another establishment of the same (or an associated) employer, where common terms and conditions are applied either generally or to relevant employees, and
- are also engaged
  - ➤ *'on like work'*, which is work of the same or a broadly similar nature and if the differences in frequency, nature and extent are not of practical importance; or
  - ➤ *'on work rated as equivalent'*, such rating being by a job evaluation study under various headings of demands made. If the method of job evaluation has treated men and women differently under any heading and but for this a woman's job would have been given equal value, the work may be rated as equivalent; or
  - ➤ *'on work of equal value'*, if the demands made on an employee under, for instance, such headings as effort, skill and decision-making are determined by a tribunal to be of equal value to those made upon an employee of the opposite sex, even though the work is not 'like work'.

Possible defence

The employer will have a defence if it can demonstrate that the variation in the compared employees' terms is due to a material factor:

- that does not involve treating one less favourably because of his or her sex; and
- if it nevertheless puts the claimant's sex at a relative particular disadvantage, that is still objectively justified (as being 'a proportionate means of achieving a legitimate aim').

Monitoring and enforcement

IIndividual enforcement and remedy are normally through application to the employment tribunal for a declaration of rights and (except in cases of equal treatment for pensions) for arrears of remuneration or for damages normally covering six years (or, in Scotland, five years). For pensions, the employer is under a duty to provide the pension scheme with the necessary funds to ensure equality.

Where an equal pay claim is successful, the tribunal must also order the 'losing' employer to do an equal pay audit, to identify and explain any other differences in pay for men and women and to set out its plans for avoiding further breaches of the equal pay laws. There is a fine of up to £5,000 for failing to do an audit.

A claim for equal pay to the employment tribunal must normally be made within six months of the end of employment.

However, an action for equal pay (breach of the statutorily implied 'equality clause' – see above) is possible in the ordinary courts, where the time limit for bringing proceedings is six years (of the alleged breach, not the termination of employment).

There is also a complaint to the tribunal about any victimisation for pursuing rights of equal pay (see Chapter 8).

Note: the code of practice, Equal Pay, issued by the Equality and Human Rights Commission (see Chapter 8) is both for the guidance of employers and for tribunals to take into account in deciding claims.

Gender Pay Gap Reporting

For each 12 months from the pay period that includes:

- for all public sector employers of 150 or more people, 31st March 2017; and
- for all private and voluntary sector employers of 250 or more people, 5th April 2017

there is an obligation to report annually on the difference between the pay of male and female employees.

Comparison is on both a mean average and a median basis, the difference being expressed as a percentage of the mean and median female rates. Calculation of mean and median rates excludes any reduced pay during periods of maternity or other family-related leave, and in some cases sick leave.

'Pay' includes basic pay, holiday pay, paid leave, maternity pay, sick pay, shift premia, area allowances, car allowances, on-call allowances, standby allowances, clothing allowances, first-aider allowances and fire warden allowances. It does not cover overtime, expenses, salary sacrifice payments, benefits in kind, redundancy pay, arrears of pay or tax credits.

For all bonuses, profit share payments, Long Term Incentive Payments and the equivalent value of share allocations awarded or made in the 12 months leading up to 31st March/5th April 2017 and each of its subsequent anniversaries, the annual report must include both the proportion of each gender group that has received them and their mean value for each gender group.

An employer must also state the number of male and female employees whose pay falls within each quartile of the organisation's overall pay range.

The report for any given year, signed by a director, must be published within 12 months of the relevant 31st March/5th April (that is, by the following 30th March/4th April), held on the organisation's website for three years and uploaded to a central government website.

An employer's failure to report will be an unlawful act.

Exceptions to the operation of a sex equality clause or rule

Differences in:

- the amounts a man and woman are eligible to receive in pension, if the difference is attributable only to the different entitlement of each under the state pension; and
- the amount of benefits or of the employer's contributions to such benefits that are based on different actuarial factors.

Provisions on the secrecy of pay

Any term in a contract of employment or policy that seeks to prevent or restrict a person from

- disclosing or seeking to disclose (to anyone) information about his or her terms of employment; or
- seeking disclosure of information from a colleague or former colleague about the colleague's terms

is unenforceable if the information disclosed or sought is or would be a 'relevant pay disclosure', which is one made to find out whether or to what extent there is a connection between pay and the existence of a particular 'protected characteristic' (see Chapter 8).

Working hours

Weekly hours

Under the Working Time Regulations (WTR), an employer should ensure that a worker (employee or contract worker) does not work more than an average of 48 hours per week. The average is normally taken over a 'rolling' 17-week period. All employers are required to keep records that are sufficient to show whether the limits on working time are being complied with.

However, an employee may enter into an 'opt-out' agreement to avoid the 48-hour restriction. This is terminable by a minimum notice of seven days and a maximum of three months.

There is no 48-hour maximum on weekly working time for those whose work is classified as 'unmeasured'. Examples of these workers are executives/ managers and family workers, such as au pairs.

Night workers

The hours of night workers should be based on an averaged maximum of eight hours per 24 over the 17-week reference period. This does not apply to people whose jobs involve continuity of care or surveillance, although they are entitled to compensatory rest periods.

All night workers have the right to a free health assessment before starting night work and at regular intervals during it. The purpose is to determine whether the person is fit to do night work.

Younger workers

People aged 15 to 18 are subject to an absolute maximum of eight hours' work a day and 40 hours per week.

Road transport

For all road transport workers there is an absolute maximum of 60 hours per week.

Rest periods

Workers are entitled to one daily rest period of 11 hours in a 24-hour period and one weekly rest period of 24 hours in a seven-day period. In addition, they are entitled to one rest break of 20 minutes during any period of six hours or more. However, different rules apply to young workers and for certain categories of night worker.

Employers can make some amendments to these obligations if they reach a collective agreement with a trade union or a workforce agreement with the elected representatives of the employees. The agreement can include changing the reference period for calculating the average working week and the provisions on rest periods.

Enforcement of rules on working hours

An employee has the right not to suffer a detriment for relying on rights under the WTR.

Enforcement of the regulations is either:

- for weekly/daily hours and night work, by the Health and Safety Executive (with the possibility of prosecution and unlimited fines); or
- for rest periods and breaks, by an employee's claim to the employment tribunal. A tribunal can award compensation that reflects any loss sustained by the employee as a result of the employer's breach of the regulations.

Holidays

Entitlement

The WTR provide that workers are entitled to a minimum of 28 days' (or 5.6 weeks') paid annual holiday, which can include bank/public holidays. This entitlement exceeds the minimum requirement of 20 days specified by the Working Time Directive (WTD) of the European Union.

In the year that the worker joined the employer, the entitlement accrues at the rate of one-twelfth per month. Entitlement for part-time workers who work less than five days per week is calculated pro rata.

The WTR do not generally provide for holidays to be carried over into the next holiday year (however, see **Entitlement accrued during absence**). And payment in lieu of holidays is generally only allowed on termination of employment.

Of course, the contract of employment can improve on the minimum entitlement. Also, different rules (on carrying over, say) can be applied to the amount of holiday above the minimum specified by the WTR.

Notification of leave

Most employers have their own rules for notification of holidays. The WTR also provide a formula: an employee must give advance notification of a period that is at least twice the length of the intended holiday. So, if the employee wants to take two weeks' leave then four weeks' notice must be given. If the employer wants to refuse the employee permission to take a period of leave, the notice required to the employee is the length of the period of leave requested (for example, two weeks in advance of a requested fortnight's leave).

An employer can also require an employee to take some or all of the minimum holiday entitlement on particular dates. For this to be valid, the employer must give notice of at least twice the length of the stipulated leave.

Entitlement accrued during absence

People on maternity leave or extended sickness absence will accrue holiday entitlement during these absences and can choose to take paid leave either during the absence (for example, when entitlement to sick pay has expired) or afterwards. This principle is derived from decisions of the Court of Justice of the European Union (CJEU) on the interpretation of the WTD. In particular, the CJEU has confirmed that employees who return in a subsequent leave year will have the right to take leave accrued earlier. This creates a superficial conflict with the United Kingdom's own prohibition on carrying over leave (see above). However, in accordance with established principles of interpretation, the UK courts and tribunals have been able to 'read words into' the WTR to make them compatible with the ECJ's rulings.

Holiday coinciding with sicknesss

The CJEU has ruled that, under the WTD, one or more days of holiday coinciding with a period of sickness, certified or otherwise properly verified, should be reinstated so that the worker can take the leave again. There is no conflict on this subject with the WTR, which do not address it at all. So UK courts and tribunals can simply adopt the CJEU's approach without even needing to read words into the WTR.

Payment for holiday

Each period of holiday falling within the first 20 days' entitlement under the WTR (the minimum requirement under the WTD – see above) must be paid in line with the worker's 'normal remuneration'.

All elements of recent wage/salary payments that are 'intrinsically linked' to the performance of contractually required duties (such as overtime, shift premia, production bonuses, commission, standby/call-out allowances) may have to be included in the calculation – often by averaging over a preceding 'reference period' - of holiday pay.

Enforcement of holiday entitlement

An employee can submit a claim to the employment tribunal if leave has been denied, or if leave has been taken but the employee has not received the appropriate payment for it.

Overpayments on holiday pay

If the employee takes more leave than the annual entitlement, the employer may recover the equivalent amount by a deduction from wages or salary only if a contractual provision or prior agreement so permits (see above).

5. Statutory employment rights – family matters

5 Statutory employment rights – family matters

Time off for antenatal care appointments

Lead parent

A pregnant employee (or agency worker) is entitled to paid time off for antenatal care. The care must be prescribed by a doctor, midwife or health visitor. After the first visit, the employer can ask for documentary evidence of pregnancy and details of appointments.

If an employment tribunal finds this time off has been unreasonably refused by the employer, it can award an amount of twice the pay for the time off concerned.

Accompanying parent

An employee (or agency worker) who is the husband, civil partner or partner of a pregnant woman, or the father or parent of an expected child has the right to unpaid time off to accompany the lead parent to two ante-natal care appointments, for up to 6.5 hours' duration on each occasion.

The employer is entitled to request verification of each appointment.

If an employment tribunal finds time off has been unreasonably refused by the employer, it can award an amount equivalent to twice the pay for the time refused (even though the right itself does not involve paid time off).

Time off for adoption appointments

Employees (or agency workers) proposing to adopt (alone or jointly with another adult) a child have the right to time off to attend adoption appointments.

'Adoption appointments' are those arranged by an adoption agency with regard to a child being placed for adoption or for fostering before adoption placement.

A single adopter can have paid time off to attend five appointments.

Joint adopters can have paid time off to attend five appointments and unpaid time off to attend on two occasions (broadly mirroring the lead and accompanying parent provisions on ante-natal care appointments – see above).

Each occasion of time off, whether paid or unpaid, should be for a maximum of 6.5 hours.

The employer can request verification of adoption appointments.

An employment tribunal can award compensation for the employer's unreasonable refusal to allow time off or failure to pay for time off.

Suspension on maternity grounds

Under designated health and safety legislation, an employee is entitled to be transferred (on the same terms and conditions of employment) from a job that might affect her health or that of the baby if:

- she is pregnant
- she has recently given birth, and/or
- she is breastfeeding.

If no suitable work is available, she must be suspended on pay for whatever period is medically certified.

Maternity leave

*Note: the rules on maternity leave that are described here apply, as the default position on the rights of a qualifying employee, unless and until they are displaced by that employee and her partner validly opting for shared parental leave (see **Shared parental leave** below).*

Qualification and scope

No employee may work for the two weeks immediately after the date of childbirth ('compulsory maternity leave').

An employee is entitled to a maternity leave period (MLP) of a maximum of 52 weeks (including compulsory maternity leave). This consists of 26 weeks' 'ordinary maternity leave' (OML) and 26 weeks' 'additional maternity leave' (AML).

To qualify for this entitlement, the employee must notify her employer, by the 15th week before her expected week of childbirth (EWOC), that she is pregnant, of the EWOC and when she wants the leave to start.

The employee can choose to start her leave at any time during the eleven weeks before the EWOC (although leave starts automatically if the employee is absent for a reason to do with pregnancy during the four weeks before the EWOC).

The employee may change the starting date of her leave, provided that she tells her employer at least 28 days in advance of that starting date, unless this is not reasonably practicable. If requested, she must provide a medical certificate that shows the expected date of childbirth.

Once the employee has notified the employer of the starting date of her leave, the employer must respond within 28 days telling the employee the date on which she is expected to return to work if she takes her full 52-week entitlement to maternity leave.

The contract of employment continues during both OML and AML and all the employee's contractual benefits, apart from pay, are maintained during the whole of her MLP. The MLP also counts as pensionable service.

Contact during maternity leave

Both the employer and employee may contact each other to discuss matters to do with work or maternity, provided that the amount or type of contact is reasonable. An employee may do up to ten 'keeping in touch' (KIT) days, doing agreed work, for an agreed rate of pay, without bringing her maternity leave to an end.

The pay for a KIT day is offset against any statutory maternity pay (see below) due for the week in which the KIT day falls.

Return to work after maternity leave

The same notice of return requirements apply both to OML and to AML.

If the employee wishes to return before the end of either OML or AML, she must give her employer at least eight weeks' notice of the date on which she wants to return. If she fails to do so, the employer can postpone her return for up to eight weeks after her request was made, as long as this does not delay her return beyond the end of the full 52-week MLP.
The employee does not have to give any notice to return on the expiry of either the 26-week OML or the 52-week MLP.

After OML, the employee has the right to return to the job she was in before her leave started, with all the rights she had, unless that is not possible because of redundancy – in which case she is entitled to be offered any suitable available vacancy before a redundancy dismissal can be fair.

After AML, she may only return to the same job if it is reasonably practicable. If it is not for a reason other than redundancy, a suitable alternative job must be offered. And if return to the same job is not possible because of redundancy, the position is as for return from OML above.

The employee may ask to return to work part-time after maternity leave (see also flexible working below). This is not within the scope of her statutory right to return (see above) and, in that sense, the employer can refuse the request. However, if the employer does so without a business justification, the woman may bring a claim for indirect sex discrimination (see Chapter 8).

If the employer refuses to allow a woman to exercise the right (whether pure or adapted as described above) to return to work after maternity leave, she will be regarded as dismissed and the dismissal will be automatically unfair. This could lead the woman to make a claim to the employment tribunal and to an award of compensation.

If a woman is found to have suffered a detriment because of pregnancy or maternity leave, an employment tribunal can award her unlimited compensation.

Statutory maternity pay

Note: the rules on maternity pay that are described here apply, as the default position on the rights of a qualifying employee, unless and until they are displaced by that employee and her partner validly opting for shared parental leave and so becoming eligible for statutory shared parental pay (see **Shared parental pay** below).

To qualify for statutory maternity pay, a woman:

- must have at least 26 weeks' continuous service (irrespective of the number of hours worked) at the start of the 15th week before the expected confinement (the 'qualifying week'); and
- must have average weekly gross earnings in the eight weeks up to and including the qualifying week that are at least equal to the lower earnings limit for National Insurance Contributions (£116.00 from April 2018); and
- still be pregnant at the 11th week before the expected confinement.

The amount of statutory maternity pay is normally 90% of average weekly earnings for each of the first 6 weeks of maternity leave, followed by 33 weeks at the flat rate (£145.18 from April 2018) or 90% of average earnings if that is less. The total of 39 weeks is known as the Maternity Pay Period (MPP).

Any pay rise applying to a woman after the start of the period used to calculate statutory maternity pay and before the end of the maternity leave period is taken into account when calculating the amount of statutory maternity pay due.

If the employee is absent for a pregnancy-related reason on or after the beginning of the fourth week before the EWOC, the MPP starts automatically.

Employers are reimbursed for statutory maternity pay. They may deduct 92% of the gross payment of statutory maternity pay from their monthly National Insurance contributions. Small employers (those whose annual National Insurance contributions are £45,000 or less) recover 100%.

Paternity leave

Note: *The rules on paternity leave described here apply, as the default position on the rights of a qualifying employee, unless and until they are displaced by that employee and their partner validly opting for shared parental leave (see* **Shared parental leave** *below).*

Qualification

An employee must:

- have, or expect to have, responsibility for the child's upbringing; and
- be the biological father of the child, or the mother's husband or partner; and
- have worked continuously for the employer for 26 weeks leading into the 15th week before the baby is due.

Paternity leave

An employee is entitled to two weeks' paternity leave (PL). The leave can be taken as two consecutive weeks or as one week. If only one week is taken, the entitlement to the second week is lost.

The leave must be taken within 56 days of the actual birth of the child, or, if the child is born early, within the period from the actual birth up to 56 days after the originally expected week of birth.

Only one period of PL may be taken, irrespective of whether more than one child is born as a result of the same pregnancy.

The employee must tell the employer of their intention to take PL by the 15th week before the baby is expected, and must also tell the employer:

- the week the baby is due
- whether they wish to take one or two weeks' leave
- when they want the leave to start.

The employer can ask the employee to provide a self-certificate as evidence of entitlement to paternity leave. HMRC has a 'model' self-certificate for this purpose.

The employee can change their mind about when they want PL to start, provided that they tell the employer at least 28 days in advance of the day they want leave to start (unless this is not reasonably practicable).

The employee's contract of employment remains in existence during PL, except for terms about wages or salary.

The employee is entitled to return to the same job after PL.

The employee is protected from suffering a detriment or unfair dismissal for reasons to do with taking, or seeking to take, PL. If the employee believes they have been treated unfairly, they can complain to the employment tribunal, irrespective of their length of service.

Statutory paternity pay

*Note: The rules on statutory paternity pay described here apply, as the default position on the rights of a qualifying employee, unless and until they are displaced by that employee and his partner validly opting for shared parental leave and so becoming eligible for statutory shared parental pay (see **Shared parental pay** below).*

During PL, statutory paternity pay (SPP) is payable for up to the maximum two weeks' leave at the same rate as applies to statutory maternity pay after the first six weeks (£145.18 from April 2018).

The means of the employer's reimbursement for statutory paternity pay is the same as for statutory maternity pay

Adoption leave

*Note: he rules on adoption leave as described here apply, as the default position on the rights of a qualifying employee, unless and until they are displaced by that employee and his or her partner validly opting for shared parental leave (see **Shared parental leave** below).*

Qualification and scope

An employee who has been matched with a child for adoption is an 'adopter'.

A sole adopter or, as part of an adult couple, a primary or lead adopter is entitled to 26 weeks' ordinary adoption leave (OAL), followed by 26 weeks' additional adoption leave (AAL) – a total of 52 weeks' leave, called the Adoption Leave Period (ALP).

To qualify for adoption leave, an employee must be newly-matched with a child for adoption by an approved adoption agency.

Adoption leave is not available when a child is not newly-matched for adoption, for example when a step-parent or foster parent is adopting a partner's child.

The adopter is required to inform the employer of the intention to take leave within seven days of notification of having been matched with a child for adoption, unless this is not reasonably practicable. The adopter must tell the employer when the child is expected to be placed and when adoption leave is to start.

The employer can ask for evidence of entitlement to adoption leave. In this case, the adopter must provide a 'matching certificate' from the adoption agency. The adopter must then give the employer 28 days' notice of the date the adoption leave is to start.

The employer has 28 days to respond in writing to an employee's notification of leave. The employer must state when the employee is expected to return to work, assuming the full entitlement to leave is taken.

An adopter can change the date on which adoption leave and Statutory Adoption Pay are to start, giving at least 28 days' notice, unless this is not reasonably practicable.

All contractual benefits, apart from pay, are maintained during the ALP.

Contact during adoption leave

Both the employer and employee may contact each other to discuss matters to do with work or adoption, provided that the amount or type of contact is reasonable. An employee may do up to ten 'keeping in touch' days, doing agreed work, for an agreed rate of pay, without bringing the adoption leave to an end. The leave period is extended by the number of days worked.

Return to work after adoption leave

An employee who wishes to return before the end of either OAL or AAL must give the employer at least eight weeks' notice of the date of return. If the employee fails to do so, the employer can postpone the return for up to eight weeks after the request was made, as long as this does not delay the employee's return beyond the end of the full 52-week ALP.

The employee does not have to give any notice to return on the expiry of either the 26 weeks' ordinary leave or the 52 weeks' full leave.

Other than when the previous job has become redundant (in which case, the employee is entitled to be offered any suitable available vacancy), an employee returning from OAL is entitled to return to their previous job where the OAL was:

■ an isolated period of leave; or
■ the last of two or more consecutive periods of statutory leave (maternity, paternity, adoption, shared parental or unpaid parental) which did not include any:
  ➤ unpaid parental leave lasting more than four weeks; or
  ➤ periods of statutory leave which, when added to other periods of statutory leave (excluding unpaid parental leave) relating to the same adoption, meant a total absence of more than 26 weeks.

When returning from a period of OAL that is not covered by these provisions or returning from AAL, the right to return to the previous job is qualified not only by redundancy (where any suitable available vacancy must be offered) but also where it is not reasonably practicable, for a reason other than redundancy, to allow the employee to revert to that job. Here, the employee must be offered another job that is suitable and appropriate.

If the employer refuses to allow an employee to exercise the right (whether absolute or adapted as described above) to return to work after adoption leave, the employee will be regarded as dismissed and the dismissal will be automatically unfair. The employee could make a claim to the employment tribunal, which may award compensation.

If an employee is found to have suffered a detriment because of adoption or adoption leave, an employment tribunal can award unlimited compensation.

Statutory adoption pay

*Note: the rules on adoption pay described here apply, as the default position on the rights of a qualifying employee, unless and until they are displaced by that employee and his or her partner validly opting for shared parental leave and so becoming eligible for statutory shared parental pay (see **Shared parental pay** below).*

Employees whose weekly average gross earnings are at least equal to the lower earnings limit for National Insurance Contributions (£116 per week from April 2018) are entitled to statutory adoption pay (SAP) for a continuous period of 39 weeks (provided that the adoption is not disrupted) at the rate of 90% of average earnings for the first six weeks and the prescribed rate, (£145.18 from April 2018) or 90% of average earnings if that is less, for the remaining weeks.

Employers are reimbursed for SAP, in the same way as for SMP (see above).

Partner leave on adoption

*Note: The rules on paternal/partner leave on adoption described here apply, as the default position on the rights of a qualifying employee, unless and until they are displaced by that employee and his or her partner validly opting for shared parental leave (see **Shared parental leave and pay** below).*

Leave

An employee with 26 weeks' continuous employment ending with the week in which his or her partner (the primary adopter) is notified of matching with the child is entitled to take two consecutive weeks' leave within 56 days of the child's (or children's) placement.

Statutory paternity pay on adoption

*Note: The rules on statutory paternity/partner pay described here apply, as the default position on the rights of a qualifying employee, unless and until they are displaced by that employee and his partner validly opting for shared parental leave and so becoming eligible for statutory shared parental pay (see **Shared parental leave and pay** below).*

The provisions for statutory paternity/partner pay on adoption are materially the same as those for statutory paternity pay (see above).

Shared parental leave

This is a scheme to allow a mother who is entitled to statutory maternity leave or a primary adopter who is entitled to statutory adoption leave to curtail that entitlement so they may share the balance of the leave with the child's other parent/adoptive parent with main responsibility for care of the child in question.

Qualification and registration

To be eligible to take SPL, the mother/primary adopter (A) must:

- have at least 26 weeks' continuous employment and still be in employment at the 15th week before the EWC or at the week of adoption matching notification;
- have a partner, the other parent/adoptive parent (B), who has worked on an employed or self-employed basis in 26 of the last 66 weeks, earning a minimum of £30 per week on average for 13 of those weeks.
- be entitled to statutory maternity or adoption leave;
- 'curtail' maternity or adoption leave, either by returning to work or by serving a 'curtailment notice';
- serve a notice of entitlement and intention to take SPL or a declaration that B has served such a notice on their employer.

To be eligible to take SPL, the other parent/adoptive parent (B) must

- satisfy the same requirement as A for continuous employment;
- have a partner, the mother/primary adopter (A), who:
  - ➤ has worked on an employed or self-employed basis in 26 of the last 66 weeks, earning a minimum of £30 per week on average for 13 of those weeks;
  - ➤ was entitled to statutory maternity or adoption leave which has been curtailed.

Note:
(1) a curtailment notice should be served at least eight weeks before the desired end of maternity or adoption leave but it cannot specify an end to maternity or adoption leave that falls within the compulsory maternity leave period of two weeks following the date of childbirth or an equivalent period in adoption cases.
(2) a notice of entitlement and intention to take SPL is non-binding, but it must nevertheless specify:
  - *the EWC and the child's date of birth or, alternatively, the date A was notified of matching for adoption and either the date that the child is expected to be placed for adoption or the date of the placement;*
  - *the start and end dates of any maternity or adoption leave taken or to be taken by A;*
  - *the total amount of SPL available;*
  - *how much SPL A and B each intend to take;*
  - *the proposed start and end dates of each spell of SPL to be taken by the person serving the notice (A or B);*

and must be served at least eight weeks before the start of the first such proposed spell. It must also identify the other parent/adoptive parent and include a declaration by them that they consent to the proposed leave.

Verification and finalisation process

On receiving a notice of entitlement and intention, an employer may (but is not obliged to) request the employee to provide, within 14 days:

- a copy of the child's birth certificate or, alternatively, one or more documents issued by the adoption agency showing its name and address,

the date A was notified of matching for adoption and the date on which the agency expects placement of the child to happen; and/or
■ the name and address of the other parent's/adoptive parent's employer.

Final notice

An employee must give their employer, at least eight weeks before the start date of any SPL - therefore, possibly at the same time as the curtailment notice and the notice of entitlement and intention (see above) - a 'period of leave notice' (PLN).

It can cover more than one planned spell of SPL, in which case it must be served at least eight weeks before the first such spell.

If given before the birth or placement for adoption, the PLN must feature:

■ a start date expressed as the date of birth or a number of days following birth or, alternatively, a number of days following placement; and
■ an end date expressed as a number of days following the birth or, alternatively, the placement.

Sequel to a PLN

Where the employee's PLN records a wish to take one continuous spell of SPL, the employer must allow it.

Where it records a wish to take two or more separate spells of SPL, the employer has a period of 14 days, beginning with the date on which the PLN was given, to:

■ consent to the spells of SPL requested;
■ propose alternative dates; or
■ refuse the spells requested without proposing alternative dates.

In the last instance, or if the employer proposes alternatives but no agreement is reached within the 14 days, the employee has the choice of:

■ taking his or her total entitlement to SPL in one continuous spell (in which case, unless, within five days of the end of the 14 day period, they notify the employer of a new start date falling at least eight weeks after the date the original PLN was served, their SPL will begin on the start date of the first spell of leave requested in that PLN); or

- withdrawing the PLN by the 15th day after it was originally served.

Notice to vary leave

Once entitled to a period of SPL (whether in continuous or discontinuous spells), an employee may serve a 'variation notice' (VN) to:

- change the start or end date of any spell of SPL (provided the VN is given at least eight weeks before both the old and new dates);
- request that separate spells of SPL become a continuous one, or vice-versa; or
- cancel a spell of notified SPL (provided the VN is given at least eight weeks before that spell is due to begin).

<u>*Note:*</u>
(1) the same conditions apply to the sequel to a VN as apply to the sequel to a PLN (see above).
(2) the minimum of eight weeks for serving a VN is replaced by 'such period as is reasonably practicable' where a child is born before the first day of the EWC and, because he or she has a start date of a spell of SPL in the eight weeks following the EWC, an employee wants to bring forward that start date so that the spell of SPL begins the same length of time after birth as it would have done had time been counted from the first day of the EWC.

Number of notices

An employee may only serve a total of three notices of leave (PLNs and VNs combined) per employer. This excludes any PLN requesting discontinuous SPL which was withdrawn on or before the 15th day after it was given and any VN served where a child was born earlier than the first day of the EWC (see above).

However, this limit may be waived and varied (increased) by agreement between the parties.

Contact during SPL

Both the employer and employee may contact each other to discuss matters to do with work and/or the leave, provided that the amount or type of contact is reasonable.

An employee may do up to 20 days' agreed work (at an agreed rate of pay) for the employer during SPL without bringing the SPL to an end. These are known as 'shared parental leave in touch' (SPLIT) days and are additional to any entitlement to KIT days (see above) when on maternity or adoption leave.

Return to work after SPL

No notice is required to return on the date(s) fixed as a consequence of the PLN.

The principal right is to return to the job occupied before absence, on rights and terms at least as favourable as if there had been no absence. Failure to allow the employee to exercise that right will normally be an unfair dismissal. However, the right is varied where:

- it is not practicable for the employee to return to the previous job by reason of redundancy. In this case, the employer must offer the employee any suitable alternative vacancy that exists (with it or with a successor or associated employer), on terms and conditions that are not substantially less favourable than those of the previous job. If this is not done, the resulting dismissal will be automatically unfair (see Chapter 10).
- The employee returns from a spell of SPL which:
  - ➤ when added to other statutory leave taken in relation to the same child, means the employee has been absent in total for more than 26 weeks; or
  - ➤ is the last of two or more consecutive periods of statutory leave in relation to the same child which included a period of parental leave of more than four weeks (see below) or a period of AML or AAL (see above).

In these two cases, if return to the original job is not reasonably practicable, the right to return becomes one to another job which is both suitable and appropriate for them.

If an employee is found to have suffered a detriment for a reason related to SPL, an employment tribunal can award unlimited compensation.

Statutory shared parental pay

Eligibility is broadly as for SPL (see above), with the additional requirement that, to qualify for shared parental pay (SHPP), any person must have weekly average gross earnings are at least equal to the lower earnings limit for National Insurance Contributions (£116 per week from April 2018).

The total entitlement to SHPP between the two parents is 39 weeks, less any weeks spent in receipt of SMP (or Maternity Allowance) or SAP.

Except in the case of a birth occurring before the first day of the EWC, SHPP cannot commence sooner than eight weeks after the relevant notifications (similar to those required for SPL – see above) have been served on the employer(s).

Entitlement to SHPP will expire:

■ after the 39-week allocation (including any SMP/Maternity Allowance or SAP) has been used up, or
■ in any event, one year after the birth or placement for adoption.

Weekly rate of SHPP is the lower of the prescribed rate (£145.18 from April 2018) or 90% of the recipient's normal weekly earnings.

Employers are reimbursed for SHPP at the rate of either 92% or, for small employers, 100%.

Flexible working requests

Scope of the right to request

The right to apply to an employer to work flexibly is open to any employee who has at least 26 weeks' continuous employment and who has not made another application to work flexibly under this right in the previous 12 months.

Nature and effect of requested changes

Employees can request:

■ a change in their hours of work
■ a change to the times when they are required to work
■ to work from home.

If a request is accepted, it will lead to a permanent change in the employee's terms and conditions of employment.

Processing a request

An employee who wishes to make an application to work flexibly must do so in writing. The application must state that it is a request for flexible working; the flexible working pattern that is applied for and the date on which the employee proposes it should start; and the effect of the change on the business and how this effect could be dealt with.

The employer has a duty to consider the request reasonably and make a decision on it within a standard period of three months (capable of extension by agreement), including any appeal that the employer allows.

An employee's application will be treated as withdrawn if the employer notifies the employee of that outcome when:

■ they failed to attend the first two meetings to discuss it; or
■ they failed to attend the first two appeal meetings (if an appeal is allowed).

Can an employer refuse an application for flexible working?

It can be refused for one, or more, of the following reasons:

■ the burden of additional costs
■ the detrimental effect on the ability to meet customers' demands
■ the inability to reorganise work among the current staff
■ the detrimental impact on quality or performance
■ an inability to recruit
■ insufficiency of work during the periods when the employee proposes to work
■ planned structural changes.

Referral to the employment tribunal

An employee may refer a complaint about a request if:

■ the employer fails to deal with the application in a reasonable manner
■ the employer fails to notify the employee of a decision within the decision period
■ the decision was based on incorrect information
■ the reason given for the refusal is not one that is specified
■ a decision to treat the application as withdrawn was not based on a specified reason (see above).

If the employee's complaint is upheld, the tribunal can order the employer to reconsider and/or to pay compensation. The maximum compensation that the tribunal can award is eight weeks' pay, at a maximum of £508 per week.

An employee has the right not to suffer a detriment, or to be dismissed, for seeking to exercise the right to request flexible working or for accompanying or seeking to accompany someone who wishes to exercise the right.

Guidance

Operation of the flexible working right is supported by a Code of Practice issued by Acas, which can be taken into account by the employment tribunal, and a supplementary Good Practice Guide.

Parental leave

*Note: The right described here is individual and is not to be confused with 'Shared parental leave' (see **Shared parental leave and pay** above).*

Scope of entitlement

An employee with one year's service is entitled to take a total of 18 weeks' unpaid parental leave for any purpose connected with the care of each child for whom the employee has parental responsibility. The right is to 18 weeks' leave in total, with all employers.

The leave must be taken before the child's eighteenth birthday.

Conditions of taking parental leave

Unless there is a separate collective agreement with a trade union or a workforce agreement with employee representatives, the following provisions apply:

- the employee must give the employer at least 21 days' notice of the intention to take parental leave and tell the employer the dates on which the leave is to start and finish
- the employee can take a maximum of four weeks' parental leave for any particular child in a particular year
- a period of leave that lasts less than a week counts as a week

- the employer has the right to postpone leave for up to six months on business grounds (except when leave is immediately after the birth of the child).

Referral to the employment tribunal

An employee who is refused the right to take parental leave, or whose employer postpones the leave unreasonably, may make a claim to the employment tribunal leading to an award of compensation.

An employee has the right not to suffer detrimental treatment by the employer for exercising the right to take parental leave.

Time off for dependants

Scope of entitlement

A 'dependant' is a spouse, child, parent or person living in the employee's household as one of the family and, for the first three situations listed below, also a person for whom the employee is the primary carer.

An employee is entitled to reasonable unpaid time off work:

- to assist a dependant who is ill, injured or assaulted, or who gives birth
- to arrange care for an ill or injured dependant
- because of unexpected problems with a dependant's care arrangement
- in consequence of a dependant's death
- to deal with an unexpected incident, during school hours, affecting a child.

The right is only available if the employee tells the employer, as soon as possible, the reason for the absence and, if practicable, how long it is expected to last

Referral to the employment tribunal

An employee who is refused time off may complain to the employment tribunal, with a possible award of compensation.

An employee has the right not to suffer detrimental treatment by the employer for exercising the right to take time off.

6. Trade union membership, duties and activities

6 Trade union membership, duties and activities

Time off

For officials

An official of a recognised independent trade union has the right to reasonable time off, with pay, for industrial relations duties and training. These must be concerned with matters that are the subject of negotiation with the employer or with other functions that the employer has recognised as appropriate for the union.

For accredited learning representatives

Accredited learning representatives of a recognised, independent union are entitled to reasonable time off, with pay, to carry out their duties (analysing the need for training, advising members on learning, arranging training for members, consulting the employer, and associated preparation) and to ensure that they are adequately trained for these functions.

For members

A member of a recognised independent union has the right to reasonable time off for union activities (not industrial action). There is no statutory right to pay for this time off.

An Acas Code of Practice, Time Off for Trade Union Duties and Activities, clarifies these rights. 'Duties' are defined and those items listed as 'activities' cannot be claimed as union duties that attract a mandatory payment.

Inducements

A worker has the right not to be induced by the employer:

- not to be a member of an independent trade union
- not to take part in the activities of an independent trade union
- not to make use of a trade union's services
- to be a member of a trade union or
- if he or she is a member of a recognised union (or one seeking recognition), to adopt terms of employment that will not be determined by a collective agreement negotiated by that union.

An employee (or worker) can complain to the employment tribunal that the employer has attempted such inducement. A successful complaint attracts an award of £4,059 (from April 2018).

Victimisation

A worker has the general right to apply to the employment tribunal claiming that an employer has taken action short of dismissal (such as withholding opportunities for transfer, training and promotion) against her or him as an individual:

- to prevent, deter or penalise the worker for membership of an independent trade union
- to prevent, deter or penalise the worker for participation in the activities of an independent trade union or for making use of its services at an appropriate time
- to compel the worker to join a union
- to penalise the worker for involvement in union recognition or derecognition (see Chapter 14)
- because of the worker's failure to accept an inducement (see above)
- because the worker features on a prohibited 'blacklist' (see Chapter 3).

The remedy is a complaint to the employment tribunal for a declaration and compensation (an amount that the tribunal considers just and equitable reparation for the loss).

The employer and/or worker can join a third party (person or trade union) who, they claim, induced the alleged victimisation by actual or threatened industrial action. The tribunal may order that third party to pay part or all of any award.

7. Miscellaneous statutory rights

7   Miscellaneous statutory rights

Health and safety

Time off

Safety representatives nominated by trade unions or elected by employees are entitled to reasonable paid time off to perform functions and undergo appropriate training.

Victimisation

An employee has the right to complain to an employment tribunal of detrimental treatment by the employer arising from the following actions by the employee:

- undertaking activities in connection with reducing risks to health and safety (having been designated by the employer to undertake such activities)
- performing functions as an acknowledged safety representative or member of a safety committee
- taking part in consultation with the employer on safety matters or in an election of employee representatives in accordance with specific regulations
- bringing to the employer's attention, by reasonable means, matters believed to be harmful to health and safety (if either there is no safety representative or committee, or it is not practicable to contact them)
- leaving or refusing to return to a place of work in circumstances of serious and imminent danger
- taking steps to protect himself or herself or others from serious and imminent danger.

In most of the above, proposed action by the employee of the type described is also protected.

The remedy is a complaint to the employment tribunal for a declaration and compensation (an amount that the tribunal considers just and equitable reparation for the loss).

Employee representatives

Time off

An employee who is an employee representative for the purposes of consultation (see Chapter 12) or a candidate for such a post, has the right to reasonable time off with pay to undertake relevant functions.

Enforcement is by a claim to the employment tribunal, which will award a successful claimant the amount of pay for the time off denied or not paid for.

Victimisation

The employee has the right not to be subjected to any detrimental treatment by his or her employer on the grounds that, as an employee representative or as a candidate in an election for that post, he or she performed, or proposed to perform, relevant functions or activities.

Enforcement is by a claim to the employment tribunal, which may award compensation based on the nature of the breach and the employee's resultant loss.

Trustees of occupational pension schemes

Time off

An employee who is a trustee of an occupational pension scheme has the right to reasonable time off with pay to perform appropriate duties or undergo relevant training.

Victimisation

An employee has the right not to be subjected to any detrimental treatment on the grounds that he or she performed or proposed to perform any relevant functions as a trustee of an occupational pension scheme in that employment.

Sunday working

"Protected' and opted-out shop workers and betting workers have the right not to be subjected to any detrimental treatment for refusing to work on Sundays. All shop workers and betting workers have the right not to be treated detrimentally for opting out or proposing to do so. The remedy is a complaint to the employment tribunal for a declaration and compensation.

Time off for public duties

The right is to reasonable time off to undertake public duties. There is no statutory right to pay for this time off. Public duties include those of a Justice of the Peace or a member of:

- a local authority
- a statutory tribunal
- a police authority
- an independent monitoring board for a prison or prison visiting committee
- a relevant health or education body
- the Environment Agency or Scottish Environment Agency
- Scottish Water or a Water Customer Consultation Panel.

'Reasonable' time off depends on the circumstances.

Jury service

An employee has the right not to be subjected to any detrimental treatment on the grounds that he or she has been summoned to attend jury service or is or has been absent from work for that purpose.

However, the employer's failure to pay the employee for such absence will not be detrimental treatment unless the contract provides for payment.

Time off when under notice of redundancy

A redundant employee with two years' continuous service is entitled to reasonable time off during the period of notice to look for work or arrange for training. The employer must pay the employee, at the appropriate rate, up to a maximum of two-fifths of a week's pay.

The employment tribunal can award two-fifths of a week's pay if it finds an employer has unreasonably refused the employee time off.

Requests for time to train

If their employers employ at least 250 people, employees with at least 26 weeks' service have the right to request time off from normal duties to undertake training that will enhance their knowledge and skills and the performance of the business.

The employer will be under a duty to consider the request according to a prescribed procedure. Key features are:

- the employee makes a written application containing information about the nature, structure and perceived purpose of the training
- within 28 days, the employer must hold a meeting to discuss the application
- within 14 days, the employer must issue a written decision, which, if it is to refuse the application, must state the grounds (broadly similar to those applying to a request for flexible working – see Chapter 5 – or that the training will not enhance the business) and confirm a right of appeal
- the employee must appeal in writing within 14 days of the decision
- the employer must arrange an appeal meeting within 14 days
- the employer must issue a decision on appeal within 14 days.

The employee has the right to be accompanied at meetings by a colleague of his or her choice.

The employee can complain to the employment tribunal about their employer's disregard of the procedure's requirements.

Disclosure in the public interest

An employee may apply to the employment tribunal for compensation if subjected to a detriment by the employer as a result of making a 'protected disclosure' of information about an alleged wrongdoing ('whistle-blowing').

The information being disclosed must be about one of the following prescribed subjects:

- a criminal offence
- a failure to comply with a legal obligation
- a miscarriage of justice
- endangering the health and safety of an individual
- damage to the environment
- concealment of any of the above.

To qualify for protection, the employee's disclosure must normally be made:

- to the employer (if a worker's employment is with people appointed by a Minister of the Crown, disclosure must be to a Minister of the Crown); or
- in the reasonable belief that one of the listed subjects is involved and that the content of the disclosure is true, to a prescribed regulatory body or a legal adviser.

Note:
(1) It is not a requirement that a disclosure be made 'in good faith' (although there is a power for the tribunal to reduce compensation for the consequences of one not in good faith). Therefore, a disclosure can be in the public interest even though the person made it for an ulterior motive.
(2) An employer can be liable for detrimental acts of other workers or its agents against a 'whistle-blower', subject to the defence of its having taken all reasonable steps to prevent such behaviour.

Data protection

Basic principles and framework

The General Data Protection Regulations (GDPR) and the Data Protection Act 2018 (DPA 2018) together create a new regime which governs the processing by data controllers of personal data relating to data subjects (concepts with which employers will be familiar from the Data Protection Act 1998).

In the employment context the data controller is the person or entity that determines the purposes and means of the processing of personal data (usually the employing entity), the data processor the person or company that processes data on behalf of the data controller and the data subject is the employee.

Personal data is 'any information relating to an identified or identifiable living individual' and that can be identified, directly or indirectly, in particular by reference to either of the following:

- an identifier such as a name, an identification number, location data or an online identifier
- one or more factors specific to the physical, physiological, genetic, mental, economic, cultural or social identity of the individual.

'
Processing data' includes collection, recording, organisation, storage, altering, retrieving, using, transmitting, combining, destroying and erasing data. Employers process personal data in respect of employees in numerous ways at all stages of employment from recruitment until after employment has ended. Data controllers are under an obligation to process data in accordance with the data principles:

- lawfulness, fairness and transparency
- purpose limitation
- data minimisation
- accuracy
- storage limitation
- integrity and confidentiality
- accountability.

Data controllers may only process personal data if one of the lawful conditions for processing is met. In an employment context this will often be one of the following conditions:

- the processing is necessary for the performance of a contract to which the data subject is party or in order to take steps at the request of a data subject prior to entering into a contract
- the processing is necessary to comply with a legal obligation to which the controller is subject
- the processing is necessary to protect the vital interests of the data subject or another person.

Certain kinds of personal data are known as 'special categories' of personal data (previously sensitive personal data under the DPA 1998, although there are some differences) and require higher levels of protection. These are racial or ethnic origin, political opinions, religious or philosophical beliefs, trade union membership, genetic data, biometric data for the purpose of uniquely identifying a natural person, health, sex life and sexual orientation. Employers need to have further justification for collecting, storing and using this type of personal information.

When processing special categories of personal data, employers must have a policy in place that explains the employer's procedures for complying with the data protection principles in connection with the processing of the data and explains the employer's policies as regards the retention and erasure of personal data processed, giving an indication of how long such personal data is likely to be retained. They must also comply with additional safeguarding requirements relating to record keeping. Employers can only process special categories of personal data in certain circumstances, including where they need to carry out their legal obligations or exercise rights in connection with employment, in some cases with explicit written consent where it is needed in the public interest (for example for equal opportunities monitoring), where it is needed in relation to legal claims or where it is needed to protect the data subject's interests (or someone else's interests) and they are not capable of giving consent.

Employees, as data subjects, have various rights under the GDPR in some circumstances to:

■ request access to their personal information (commonly known as a 'data subject access request')
■ request correction of the personal information that is held about them
■ request erasure of their personal information
■ object to processing of their personal information
■ request the restriction of processing of their personal information
■ request the transfer of your personal information to another party.

Employers need to make employees aware of their rights under the GDPR. Most employers process data, which means that they must be registered with the Information Commissioner as doing so.

Employees' access to their personal data

Employees are entitled to see what data are held on them, provided that their requests are made in writing. Access to the data must normally be given within one month of the request although the employer may extend that period by two months where necessary, taking into account the complexity and number of requests. If the data identify a third person, the employee does not have an automatic right to see those data. Either the consent of the third party must first be obtained, or identifying features must be removed.

References

There is no general legal duty to provide a reference about an employee or ex-employee. Employers should, however, be mindful of any potential claim for victimisation, during or after employment, under the various laws against discrimination (see Chapter 8).

When a reference is provided, there is a legal duty of care, both to the person it is about and to the person it is being sent to. This requirement can be met if the reference is factual and fair.

Being accompanied at disciplinary and grievance hearings

The right

A worker has the right, on reasonable request, to be accompanied at any grievance or disciplinary hearing by a work colleague or trade union representative.

A grievance hearing is a meeting to discuss a failure by an employer to perform a duty owed to a worker.

A disciplinary hearing is one which could result in:

■ a formal warning or some other action; or
■ the confirmation of a warning or other action (that is, an appeal).

A hearing should be postponed for a maximum of five days if the chosen companion cannot attend.

The limits of the companion's role

The companion (who must be allowed paid time off work) is permitted:

- to put the worker's case
- to sum up that case
- to respond on the worker's behalf to any view expressed at the hearing (but not to answer questions on behalf of the worker).

What if the employer refuses to allow the worker to be accompanied?

The remedy is a complaint to the employment tribunal and an award of up to two weeks' pay (at a maximum of £508 per week). Also, a worker may seek compensation from the employment tribunal if subjected to a detriment for exercising the right to be accompanied or for acting as the companion of another worker.

Note: the requirement for a worker's accompaniment request to be 'reasonable' does not allow the employer to refuse accompaniment by a particular colleague chosen by the worker.

The Acas Code of Practice on disciplinary and grievance procedures

This provides practical guidance and sets out the principles for handling matters of discipline and grievance. The employment tribunal will take the code into account when considering relevant cases. It can adjust any award by up to 25% for unreasonable failure to comply with the code. So, if the tribunal feels that an employer has unreasonably failed to follow the guidance in the code, it can increase an award. If it feels an employee has failed to follow the guidance, it can reduce any award by up to 25%.

Medical reports

For employment or insurance reasons, an employer may obtain a report from a medical practitioner who is responsible for the clinical care of an employee. Before the employer can get the report, the employee must be told that the employer is to apply for the medical information and the employee must give consent.

The employee must also be told his or her rights to do with the report. These are:

- to withhold consent to the application for the report or the disclosure of its contents
- to see the report before it is given to the employer
- to ask for a copy of the report within six months of its supply
- to amend any part of the report that he or she considers inaccurate or misleading.

A medical practitioner may refuse to allow a person to see a report if doing so would cause serious physical or mental harm, or would reveal the identity of someone who has supplied information for the report.

An employee who refuses consent for a medical report could be made subject to disciplinary action and/or the withdrawal of sick pay. Any decision by the employer about the employee's suitability for continued employment or for a particular type of work will have to be taken on the basis of other information available.

Note: for pre-employment requests for medical information, see Chapters 3 and 8.

Zero-hours workers

It is unlawful for an employer to subject a ZHW to any detrimental treatment for breaching an exclusivity clause in a ZHC or ZHA (see Chapter 2).

A successful complaint to the employment tribunal will result in an award of compensation that is just and equitable in the circumstances.

8. Equality, diversity and non-discrimination

8   Equality, diversity and non-discrimination

Laws promoting diversity

Legislation protects people in work from being subjected to 'prohibited conduct' to do with a 'protected characteristic'.

Generally, the intention of the alleged perpetrator is irrelevant to whether or not prohibited conduct has occurred.

Protected characteristics

These are:

- Sex – being male or female.
- Sexual Orientation – whether towards others of the same sex, the opposite sex or both sexes.
- Marriage or civil partnership (but not being single).
- Gender reassignment/transsexuality – the person is undergoing, has undergone or is proposing to undergo all or part of a process to reassign sex by changing physiological or other attributes of sex (Note: the process does not have to be a 'medical' one).
- Race – including colour, nationality, and ethnic or national origins
- Religion or belief – any religion or 'religious or philosophical belief' or the lack of one.
- Disability – a physical or mental impairment that has a substantial and long-term (having lasted or being likely to last for 12 months or the rest of life) adverse effect on the ability to carry out normal day-to-day activities. Also note:
  - ➤ the effect of impairment must be judged without regard to medical treatment or other corrective aids or measures
  - ➤ a progressive condition that is likely ultimately to have the required effect is treated as a disability even though it has not yet reached that stage
  - ➤ recurring conditions that have the required effect are treated as continuing to have that effect during periods of remission
  - ➤ severe involuntary disfigurements, blindness, partial sightedness, cancer, HIV and multiple sclerosis are automatically treated as disabilities
  - ➤ a disability that has now ceased can still be a protected characteristic.

- Age – being either of a particular age or within a particular range of ages.
- Pregnancy and maternity – the protected period between the start of pregnancy and, for an employee, the expiry of the AML (see Chapter 5) or, if earlier, return to work after pregnancy or, for a non-employee, the expiry of two weeks after the end of pregnancy.

General forms of prohibited conduct

The legislation describes various types of conduct (an act or omission) by reference to a protected characteristic (see above) which, when occurring in the context of work (see below), will be unlawful. The forms of prohibited behaviour or conduct are:

Direct discrimination

Because of a protected characteristic, A treats B less favourably than A treats or would treat others.

Note:
(1) *The wording of the definition allows it to cover situations in which B does not have the protected characteristic but A's treatment of B is either (i) because A perceives B to have it or (ii) because B associates with others (except spouses or civil partners and, possibly, those who are pregnant) who do have it.*
(2) *If the protected characteristic is age, there is a defence of justification (if the conduct in question is a 'proportionate means of achieving a legitimate aim').*
(3) *If the protected characteristic is disability and B is not disabled, there is no direct discrimination simply because A treats disabled people more favourably than B.*

Indirect discrimination

There are three necessary elements:

- A applies a 'provision, criterion or practice' which puts or would put those with whom B shares a protected characteristic at a particular disadvantage compared with those with whom B does not share it
- it puts or would put B at that disadvantage, and
- A cannot justify it as a proportionate means of achieving a legitimate aim.

<u>Note:</u> *the protected characteristic of pregnancy and maternity (see above) is not specifically within the scope of indirect discrimination, although the protected characteristic of sex is, and would cover most pregnancy/maternity anyway.*

Harassment

There are three forms:

- A engages in unwanted conduct to do with sex, sexual orientation, gender reassignment, race, religion or belief, disability or age and the conduct has the purpose or effect of violating B's dignity or of creating an intimidating, hostile, degrading, humiliating or offensive environment for B
- A engages in unwanted conduct of a sexual nature and the conduct has the same effect or purpose
- A or another engages in unwanted conduct to do with sex or gender reassignment or of a sexual nature that has the same effect or purpose and then, because B rejects that conduct, A treats B less favourably than would otherwise have been the case.

<u>Note:</u> *In all three forms of harassment, the effect of the conduct must be judged with reference to B's perception, to the other circumstances, and to whether it is reasonable for the conduct to have that effect.*

Victimisation

A subjects B to a detriment because B has done, or because A believes B has done or may do, one of the following:

- bringing legal proceedings about a protected characteristic
- giving evidence or information in connection with such proceedings
- making an allegation that someone has broken the law on equality (including equal pay – see Chapter 4).

Note: there is no need for a comparator here.

Instructing, causing or inducing discrimination or other prohibited conduct

A instructs, causes, induces or attempts to cause or induce B to undertake prohibited conduct affecting C.

Aiding discrimination or other prohibited conduct

A knowingly helps B to discriminate or undertake prohibited conduct (unless A reasonably relies on a statement by B that the conduct for which help is given is not unlawful).

Work-based situations in which discrimination will normally be unlawful

'Employment'

Prohibited conduct (particularly discrimination and victimisation) will generally be unlawful, so, as applicable, an employee, worker (operating under a contract to do work personally – see Chapter 2) or job applicant will be allowed to take action against the 'employer' if such conduct exists in:

- the operation of the arrangements for selection
- a refusal or deliberate omission to offer employment
- the terms of employment offered
- the terms operated/applied in employment
- access to opportunities for promotion, transfer or training; or to benefits, facilities or services or
- dismissal or other detriment.

<u>Note:</u>

(1) *Direct discrimination that occurs in selection, recruitment, promotion/ transfer/training or dismissal will not be unlawful if having a particular protected characteristic is an 'occupational requirement' for a job and the exercise of that requirement is justified as being a proportionate means of achieving a legitimate aim.*

(2) *Acts of discrimination or harassment that occur after employment has ended are unlawful if they arise out of and are closely connected with the previous employment.*

'Contract (or agency) workers'

Those hired out by their employer to a host business for which they do work (see also Chapter 2) are protected against harassment by the host. They are also protected against discrimination and victimisation by the host:

- in the terms on which the host allows the workers to do the work
- in not allowing the worker to do or to continue doing the work
- in access to opportunities for receiving a benefit, facility or service
- in any other detriment.

Issues and exemptions linked to particular protected characteristics

Sex

Exemptions are:

- discrimination, based on reasonable reliance on reputable actuarial or other data, in an annuity, life insurance policy, accident insurance policy or similar thing involving the assessment of risk
- discrimination on matters covered separately by the equal pay provisions (see below and Chapter 4)
- discrimination that is necessary to comply with statutory provisions to protect women against risks specific to them, such as pregnancy and maternity.

Marriage/civil partnership

- Exempted is discrimination based on reasonable reliance on reputable actuarial or other data, in an annuity, life insurance policy, accident insurance policy or similar thing involving the assessment of risk.

Gender reassignment

■ A specific form of unlawful discrimination applies here if, on B's absence because of gender reassignment (perhaps for a medical procedure or counselling), A treats B less favourably than A would if B's absence:
  ➤ were because of sickness or injury; or
  ➤ were for some other reason and it was not reasonable for B to be treated less favourably.
■ Exempted is discrimination based on reasonable reliance on reputable actuarial or other data, in an annuity, life insurance policy, accident insurance policy or similar thing involving the assessment of risk.

Religion or belief

Your belief / my belief

To be a 'protected characteristic', a 'belief' does not have to be religious in nature or foundation. It must be:

■ genuinely held
■ a belief, not an opinion or viewpoint
■ a belief about a weighty and substantial aspect of human life and behaviour
■ able to attain a certain cogency, seriousness, cohesion and importance
■ worthy of respect in a democratic society; not incompatible with human dignity; and not in conflict with the fundamental rights of others.

So, for example, it has been held that a claimant's belief that mankind is heading towards catastrophic climate change and that people should live their lives in a way that would reduce or avoid that catastrophe fell within the limits of what might constitute a philosophical belief and qualify for protection.

There is an exemption for anything necessarily done pursuant to a requirement of legislation or to a requirement or condition imposed under legislation.

Disability

- If B is not disabled, there is no direct discrimination (see above) simply because A treats disabled people more favourably.
- Discrimination arising from disability.

There is an additional type of prohibited conduct where A treats B unfavourably because of something 'arising in consequence of' B's disability and A cannot justify the treatment (as a proportionate means of achieving a legitimate aim).

Note:
(1) Under this type of prohibited conduct, there is no need for a comparator of any type – so unfavourable/detrimental treatment (such as a warning or dismissal) of B for absence in consequence of a disability will be discrimination by A (unless it can be justified).
(2) There can be no discrimination here unless A knows or ought reasonably to know of B's disability.

- 'Reasonable adjustments'
  An employer has a duty, applying to all work-related situations (see above), to make reasonable adjustments if:
  ➤ a 'provision, criterion or practice'
  ➤ a physical feature of premises, or
  ➤ the absence of an auxiliary aid

places a disabled person at a substantial disadvantage to a person who is not disabled.

The duty does not arise unless the employer knows or ought reasonably to know that there is a person with a specific disability.

The duty is to take such steps as are reasonable to avoid the disadvantage or, in the third case above, to provide the auxiliary aid.

Steps might be alterations to premises, re-allocation of duties, altering hours, permitting absence during working hours, providing or modifying equipment, changing testing or assessment procedures, or making a reader or interpreter available.

Factors determining whether an employer should make an adjustment include: its effectiveness, practicability and cost.

Note:
(1) If premises are occupied by the employer under a tenancy that prohibits or restricts an alteration by the employer that would be a reasonable adjustment, the tenancy is deemed altered to stipulate:
- *that the employer is entitled to make the alteration with written consent and is obliged to apply in writing for that consent and*
- *that the landlord will not withhold consent unreasonably (but may make it subject to reasonable conditions)*
- *if the employer does not apply for the landlord's consent, that anything in the tenancy preventing alteration will be disregarded in deciding whether the employer has complied with the duty on reasonable adjustments.*
(2) If premises are occupied by the employer subject to a mortgage, charge or covenant that requires the consent of another to make an alteration that would be a reasonable adjustment, the absence of that consent will be a defence to breach of the duty provided that the employer has requested consent.

Compliance with the duty to make reasonable adjustments may entail giving a suitably qualified, disabled person priority over a better-qualified, non-disabled person (in essence, a form of 'positive discrimination').

Failure to comply with the duty on reasonable adjustments is unlawful discrimination.

■ Pre-offer enquiries about health
A should not ask about the health of B, a job applicant, before offering work to B or including B on a shortlist for selection, unless it is necessary:
➤ to establish whether B will be able to undergo an assessment or whether A will be subject to a duty to make reasonable adjustments (see above) for B to undergo an assessment
➤ to establish whether B will be able to perform a function 'intrinsic to' the work concerned
➤ to monitor diversity in job applicants
➤ to take positive action
➤ (if the work requires people with a particular disability), to establish whether B has that disability.

Contravention is enforceable by the Equality and Human Rights Commission (EHRC) (see below).

Also, if A acts in reliance on the information given about B's health, there will be a presumption of direct discrimination (see above) in any such claim brought by B. So, provided that B is a disabled person, the burden of proof will be on A to show that B was not rejected because of that.

Note: This provision does not, as such, prohibit an offer of employment subject to the receipt of a satisfactory medical reference or the completion of a satisfactory medical examination (see Chapter 3). However, if a disability were revealed by such a reference or examination, any rejection, withdrawal of the offer or (if employment had commenced) termination in reliance on that information would usually be direct discrimination.

■ Exempted from disability discrimination generally is anything necessarily done pursuant to a requirement of legislation or to a requirement or condition imposed under legislation

Age

■ As mentioned earlier, there is, uniquely within direct discrimination for the protected characteristics, a defence of justification ('a proportionate means of achieving a legitimate aim').
■ Exceptions from unlawful discrimination are:
  ➤ the quantification of benefits (such as paid holidays) by reference to a period of service of up to five years. Thereafter, any continuing lower benefit must be justified as fulfilling a 'business need'
  ➤ the provision of enhanced redundancy payments, provided that the employer uses the statutory redundancy payment as the initial basis of calculation
  ➤ anything necessarily done pursuant to a requirement of legislation
  ➤ the provision of life assurance until normal retirement age to employees taking early retirement on grounds of ill-health, or of facilities or arrangements for the care of children of a particular age group
  ➤ the operation of certain age-based rules, criteria or decisions on pensions.

Pregnancy/maternity

- As indicated earlier, a claim of indirect discrimination involving this protected characteristic cannot be made.
- There is a specific additional protection against discrimination by A against B if:
  - ➤ in the protected period of B's pregnancy (see earlier), A treats her unfavourably because of the pregnancy or illness resulting from it; or
  - ➤ A treats her unfavourably because she is on compulsory maternity leave (see Chapter 5).

  It is worth noting that:
  - ➤ because of the wording, there is no need for a male or non-pregnant comparator but there is arguably no scope for an associative pregnancy/ maternity discrimination claim (which instead would have to be brought under the general direct discrimination definition – see above)
  - ➤ if pregnancy-related or maternity-related treatment occurred outside the times specified, a claim would have to be brought under the general direct discrimination definition (see above).
- Exceptions are:
  - ➤ discrimination, based on reasonable reliance on reputable actuarial or other data, in an annuity, life insurance policy, accident insurance policy or similar thing involving the assessment of risk
  - ➤ discrimination that is necessary to comply with statutory provisions to protect women against risks specific to them, such as pregnancy and maternity
  - ➤ removing during maternity leave any benefit of non-contractual pay (except any bonus for times when the woman is on compulsory maternity leave and any bonus for performance during a time she was at work).

Liability for unlawful acts (for any protected characteristic)

An employer will be (vicariously) liable for prohibited conduct by its employees or agents, unless it is able successfully to rely on the defence of having taken reasonably practicable steps to prevent the unlawful act (for example, by issuing policies on, or providing training in, diversity).

The 'guilty' employees or agents can be personally liable, whether or not the employer has relied on its defence and whether or not any such reliance has been successful. There is no requirement here (as there generally is when discrimination is aided – see above) that the employee or agent acted knowingly. However, the employee or agent can still escape liability if it is shown that the prohibited conduct was undertaken in reasonable reliance on a statement by the employer that the act concerned was not unlawful.

Promotion, guidance and enforcement (for any protected characteristic)

Positive action

There is protection against possible discrimination claims for employers who take proportionate measures to increase job applications from those with a specific protected characteristic that is under-represented or to address through training and advice disadvantages experienced by a specific group.

Public sector equality duty

There is a requirement for a public authority to have due regard to the need to eliminate prohibited conduct, advance equality of opportunity and foster good relations between different groups.

In advancing equality of opportunity, a public authority should have particular regard to removing or minimising disadvantages that are connected to a particular protected characteristic and to taking steps to meet the unique needs of those with a particular protected characteristic.

Enforcement is only by way of judicial review through interested people or by EHRC (see below).

Code of Practice

See the 'Employment' code of practice, issued by EHRC. Its provisions can be taken into account by an employment tribunal (see below).

The Equality and Human Rights Commission

EHRC performs other enforcement and educational functions. It has the powers to investigate, to obtain information, to issue notices of unlawful acts (perhaps with an action plan), to apply for an injunction against persistent offenders, to provide legal assistance and to apply for a declaration of rights.

Application to the employment tribunal

This must be made within three months of the act complained of, but a tribunal may admit an 'out of time' case, if it considers it 'just and equitable' to do so. Conciliation from Acas is always available. The tribunal has three possible remedies:

■ a declaration: a statement of the rights of the claimant and in what respect the employer or any employee has acted unlawfully
■ compensation: an uncapped amount for any financial losses (including future loss) and for injury to feelings
■ recommendations: to benefit the employee and lessen the effect of the discrimination.

Injured feelings

An employment tribunal can award compensation for 'injury to feelings' in discrimination cases. The so-called 'Vento guidelines' were first established in 2002 and have since been updated to take account of inflation. There are three bands, most recently:

■ £25,700-£42,900 for the most serious cases, such as a lengthy campaign of harassment. An award of more than £42,900 would be exceptional
■ £8,600-£25,700 for serious cases that do not merit the highest band
■ £900-£8,600 for less serious cases, such as an isolated act of discrimination. The guidelines say awards of less than £900 should be avoided.

In determining fair and reasonable compensation, tribunals are advised to have regard to the 'overall magnitude of the sum total of compensation for non-pecuniary loss made under the various headings of injury to feelings, psychiatric damage and aggravated damage'.

Discrimination against part-time workers

Coverage and nature of protection

A part-time worker is one with hours of work that are less than those of a full-time worker employed by the same employer, doing the same work and having the same type of contract. (So, strictly, someone who works 35 hours a week rather than the full 37.5 normally required would be a part-timer.)

Part-time workers have the right not to be treated less favourably than a 'comparable' full-time worker, unless the employer can justify that treatment. This covers terms and conditions of employment (usually 'pro rata' equality is required) or any other detriment.

Taking action

Employees have the right to request from the employer a written explanation if they believe they are being treated less favourably than a comparable full-time employee. The employer must respond within 21 days. Deliberate and unreasonable failure to reply, or evasive or equivocal answers, can lead to the inference of discrimination.

The remedy is a complaint of discrimination to the employment tribunal, which may make a declaration and/or an award of compensation. There is also protection against victimisation for relying on these rights.

Discrimination against fixed-term employees

Coverage and basic nature of the protection

A 'fixed-term contract' is one that terminates on the expiry of a period, on the completion of a particular task or on the occurrence or non-occurrence of a specified event. A contract with one of these features remains a 'fixed-term contract' even if it contains a provision for earlier termination by the giving of notice. Some legislation refers to the same range of contracts as 'limited-term contracts' (see Chapter 3).

Employees on fixed-term contracts ('fixed-term employees') should not be treated less favourably than comparable, 'permanent' employees on the grounds that they are fixed-term employees, unless this is objectively justified.

Treatment of fixed-term employees

Fixed-term employees can compare themselves with employees of the same employer who are not on fixed-term contracts and who do the same or broadly similar work. If there is no comparable 'permanent' employee in the establishment, a comparison can be made with a similar permanent employee working for the employer in a different establishment.

Treatment may be assessed against either:

- any one of the fixed-term employee's terms and conditions of employment, which should be not less favourable than the comparable 'permanent' employee's, or
- the fixed-term employee's overall package of terms and conditions of employment, which should not be less favourable than that of the comparable 'permanent' employee.

What if fixed-term employees feel they are being treated unfairly?

Employees have the right to request from the employer a written explanation if they believe they are being treated less favourably than a comparable 'permanent' employee. The employer must respond within 21 days. Deliberate and unreasonable failure to reply, or evasive or equivocal answers, can lead to the inference of discrimination.

Limitation on successive contracts

The use of successive fixed-term contracts is limited to four years' service, unless the use of further fixed-term contracts is justified on objective grounds. So, if there is no such justification, a fixed-term contract renewed after the four-year period of service will be treated as a contract for an indefinite period.

Waiver clauses

Any clause that still exists in a fixed-term contract that purports to deny or waive the right to claim unfair dismissal and/or to claim a statutory redundancy payment on the expiry of that contract without renewal (which is a dismissal – see Chapter 10) is now invalid.

Access to permanent work

Fixed-term employees should be given information on permanent vacancies in the organisation.

Referral to the employment tribunal

The remedy is a complaint of discrimination to the employment tribunal for a declaration and/or compensation. There is also protection against victimisation for relying on rights.

Discrimination against convicted offenders

'Spent' convictions

After a period of good behaviour (unless stated otherwise, after the end of the sentence), a conviction is 'spent' – that is, treated as if it had never occurred. Rehabilitation periods (with one separately bracketed for those aged under 18 when found guilty) are:

■ Custodial sentence of more than 4 years	Never spent
■ Custodial sentence of more than 2.5 years up to 4 years	7 (3.5) years
■ Custodial sentence of between 6 months and 2.5 years	4 (2) years
■ Custodial sentence of 6 months or less	2 (1.5) years
■ Community/Youth Rehabilitation Order	1 (0.5) year
■ Fine [from date of conviction]	1 (0.5) year
■ Conditional discharge, Referral/Reparation Order	Period of order
■ Absolute discharge	None

Job applicants are not obliged to disclose spent convictions, the intention being that these should not be used as grounds for discrimination in recruitment, during employment, or as reason for dismissal.

Note: it is a criminal offence to require a job applicant or employee to use a subject access request to get a copy of their own criminal record – which will include spent convictions – in connection with their recruitment or continued employment (a practice known as enforced subject access).

However, there is no specific individual protection or remedy for breach of the general principle that no reliance should be placed upon spent convictions, except when someone with the requisite length of service is dismissed and can claim unfair dismissal (see Chapter 10).

Exceptions

Among the jobs where applicants must disclose all convictions, regardless of whether they are spent or not, are medical practitioner, vet, nurse, lawyer, accountant, police officer, traffic warden, teacher, social worker and youth worker; but not security worker

9. Changes to the employment relationship

9   Changes to the employment relationship

Changing the identity of the employer

Application of the law on transfer of undertakings (TUPE)

Under legislation, commonly known as TUPE, employees' rights are safeguarded when there is a 'relevant transfer' of a business or undertaking, or part of it, to a new employer. A 'relevant transfer' is either:

- the transfer (not necessarily by sale) of all or part of a business or undertaking if that 'economic entity retains its identity' and/or
- a 'service provision change' (covering contracting-out by a 'client', change of contractors after retendering, and contracting-in by a 'client'), where the service is provided by an 'organised grouping of employees'.

Transfers by acquisition of shares are excluded, because there is no change in the legal personality of the employer. However, actions by the new owner of the shareholding might result in a TUPE transfer, either conscious (where the business and employees of the newly-acquired company are then moved over to one of the owner's associated companies – see below) or otherwise (where the new shareholder intervenes in the day-to-day operations of the new acquisition to an extent that means its business has been transferred to a new controlling entity in reality).

An 'intra-group transfer' - the passing of an 'economic entity' (for example, a discrete division, department or function) between two subsidiaries in the same 'group' - will generally come within TUPE because the corporate identity of the employer does change.

Normal automatic continuation of employment contracts

In the absence of an employee's objection to transfer (see below), the contract of employment of someone employed at the time of a transfer does not terminate on the change of employer. It automatically continues as if it had been made with the new employer ('transferee').

The transferee takes over the employment/contractual liabilities of the old employer ('transferor'), with the exception of:

■ where the contract has an express incorporation clause (see Chapter 3), the obligation to give effect to any post-transfer pay increases collectively agreed by the transferor; and
■ rights under an occupational pension scheme where they relate to benefits for old age, invalidity, or survivors; and
■ criminal liabilities.

This 'automatic continuation' effect applies to an employee who was dismissed before the transfer but for a transfer-related reason that is unfair (see Chapter 10). In that case the liability for the unfair dismissal passes to the new employer.

However, the 'automatic continuation' effect is excluded, along with the specific provisions on dismissal (see above and Chapter 10), if the transferor is the subject of bankruptcy or similar insolvency proceedings that have commenced with a view to the liquidation of assets (therefore, not all insolvency situations – in particular, transferors in administration do not come within the exception).

Informing and consulting employee representatives

Before a transfer, the transferor and transferee should, under TUPE itself, each inform (and, only if measures are envisaged for their own employees, consult) representatives of its own employees affected by the forthcoming transfer (see Chapter 12).

There is also the option for the transferee, before it becomes the employer of the affected employees, undertaking pre-transfer 'collective consultation' on 20+ proposed post-transfer redundancies (also see Chapter 12).

Employee liability information for the new employer

Also, the transferor must supply the transferee with 'employee liability information' in writing at least 28 days before the transfer or, otherwise, as soon as reasonably practicable.

The employee liability information must cover:

- the identity and age of transferring employees
- information covered by their statements of employment particulars
- details of any applicable collective agreements
- disciplinary and grievance cases in the preceding two years
- legal actions in the preceding two years and ones that are reasonably expected.

The information must be accurate to a specified date no more than 14 days before it is communicated. Subsequent changes must be notified by the transferor. The information may be provided in instalments and/or through a third party.

Note: as it is required by law, the disclosure of these details under TUPE does not, in itself, result in a breach of the laws on data protection (see Chapter 7).

A transferee's remedy for the transferor's failure to comply with the obligation is a complaint to the employment tribunal, which can award compensation (normally a minimum of £500 for each employee in respect of whom relevant information was not given or was deficient).

The effect of objecting to a transfer

In a TUPE situation, if an employee objects to transferring to the new employer, the contract of employment does not transfer and, unless the transferor chooses to continue employment through redeployment, the effect is to terminate the contract.

Generally, that termination of employment will not amount to a dismissal and the employee will not be entitled to any notice, severance pay or compensation. However, there could be legal liability if the employee's objection to transferring was caused by the transferee's proposal or intention to make detrimental changes to terms and conditions.

Pension scheme arrangements

Although liability for occupational pension scheme provisions so far as they relate to benefits for old age, invalidity or survivorship do not transfer under TUPE, under pension legislation transferring employees who were offered an occupational pension scheme by the old employer must be offered any one of the following types of scheme by the new employer:

- defined benefit (if the transferee chooses this option, the scheme must comply with minimum standards)
- defined contribution ('money purchase') or
- stakeholder.

Transferee employers choosing to offer a defined contribution or stakeholder scheme must match the employees' contributions to a maximum of 6% of earnings.

Rights under an occupational pension scheme where they do not relate to benefits for old age, invalidity, or survivors (often known as 'Beckmann liabilities') do transfer.

Note: arrangements under a Group Personal Pension Plan are not covered by these rules. A transferee will be obliged contractually to continue with the pre-transfer level of contribution, even if that exceeds 6%. Contractual obligations on an employer to contribute to a personal pension are also not covered by these rules and that obligation will transfer along with other contractual terms.

Changes to terms and conditions of transferred employees

Changes made for the sole or principal reason of a transfer are void unless they are:

- by agreement and for an 'economic, technical or organisational reason entailing changes in the workforce' (change in number of jobs, content of jobs or location of jobs);or
- permitted for the employer to make by a term of the contract; or
- to terms incorporated from a collective agreement (see Chapter 3), put into effect more than one year after the transfer and, following that, the employee's 'package' is no less favourable to them overall.

> **Changing terms on transfer – even money is not necessarily the answer**
>
> A change in a contractual term that is strongly 'transfer-related' will often be void. In one case, after a TUPE transfer and as part of a deal to retain the employee, the new employer inserted a non-compete clause into the contract. The employee later challenged the clause, which was held to be 'transfer-related' and so void, even though the employer had given the employee a 'consideration' of £65,000 for its inclusion in the contract.

Less stringent requirements apply on changing the terms of the employees of an insolvent undertaking, if the changes have the purpose of ensuring survival and safeguarding opportunities for employment.

Changing the content of the contract: terms and conditions

How a change can be made

Broadly, there are three possible approaches in practice. They are:

- Mutual agreement between employer and employee:
  - ➤ on an ad hoc basis, when the need arises; or
  - ➤ through a 'standing' clause in the contract, allowing a party (generally, the employer) to amend content.

  This is based on the principle that, just as the contract is established by agreement, so it can be varied in the same way (subject to limitation under TUPE – see above) without there being a breach of contract.
- Unilateral implementation:
  - ➤ under contractual authority (effectively, the same as above – therefore, there would be no breach of contract); or
  - ➤without contractual authority – a clear breach of contract.
- Termination of the current contract with due notice and the offer of its immediate replacement with a new contract containing the revised term(s). Here, although the specific change might not have been agreed, there will be no breach of contract because the first contract is brought to an end in accordance with its own terms (the notice clause). But, technically, the ending of the first contract does amount to a dismissal, which could have certain consequences (see below).

Other legal consequences

If the change involves both a breach of contract and the loss of a financial amount (for example, a reduction in pay), the employee will have the right to sue for any lost amount(s) falling due for payment while the contract continues in being. The employee's action might be either for damages in the County or High Courts or for one or more unlawful deductions from 'wages' in the employment tribunal (see Chapter 4).
A breach of contract will, if sufficiently serious, also entitle the employee to resign and to treat himself or herself as 'constructively' dismissed (see Chapter 10).

Dismissals resulting from a change – statutory implications

Any dismissal involved in the change, whether 'constructive' (see above) or by termination effected directly by the employer, whether in breach of contract or not (see above), may still not be 'unfair' (see Chapter 10) if the reason for the change is sufficiently important for the business ('some other substantial reason') and there has been prior consultation with the employee in an attempt to obtain agreement to the change. However, in the absence of either of these elements, it will be unfair and will allow the employee to receive compensation for financial loss, even if the employee accepted an offer of continued employment under a new contract.

Where the underlying reason for the change resulting in a dismissal is a decline in the employer's need for a particular type of work, the employee may also receive a redundancy payment (see Chapter 11).

Changes that might affect 20 or more employees

If the change is intended to affect 20 or more employees (currently, only if they are at a single 'establishment'), there will also be the requirement for the employer to consult with employee representatives about proposed dismissals for redundancy (see Chapter 12). The definitions of 'redundancy' and 'proposed dismissal' under this particular law are sufficiently wide to include almost any wide-scale change to contracts of employment, regardless of its underlying reason.

10. Terminating the contract

10   Terminating the contract

Notice entitlement

The statutory minimum notice due, on dismissal, to an employee with at least one month's continuous service is:

- one week's notice if he or she has been employed for less than two years
- one week's notice for each year of continuous employment between two years and 11 years
- 12 weeks' notice for 12 or more years' continuous employment.

The statutory minimum notice due from an employee (on resignation) is one week.

If the contractual notice is greater than the applicable statutory minimum, the contractual notice prevails.

Common misconception (2)

'....an employee's notice of resignation can be refused'

It cannot, just as an employee cannot reject the employer's notice of dismissal. Of course, you can try to persuade employees to stay. Alternatively, you can relieve them of the obligation to work out their notice and pay them off. Or, if your concern is about their joining a competitor, you can rely on any enforceable contractual provisions restraining post-termination activity or about 'garden leave'.

If an employee gives notice of resignation while facing a charge of serious misconduct, an employer is fully entitled to continue with the disciplinary process during the period of notice – only a resignation with instant effect can stop that.

If notice is worked, the employee is entitled to all contractual payments and benefits (unless the contract itself expressly withdraws them during a notice period). And if the contractual notice required from the employer does not exceed the applicable statutory minimum by more than six days, the employee has the statutory right to full pay for any day in the period of notice when he or she is absent through sickness, pregnancy, maternity/paternity/adoption leave or a lack of work and would not otherwise be entitled to full pay (for example, if sick, when the employee's entitlement to sick pay has expired).

Exactly when is 'notice' of termination given?

Regardless of the required contractual or statutory length, 'notice' is a very particular, if often basic, thing. It contains a specific date, or the information necessary to calculate the specific date, on which the contract of employment will terminate.

A mere intimation of possible dismissal or confirmation of a decision to dismiss at some unspecified time in the future, even if the broad period during which the dismissal will probably occur is stated, will not amount to the giving of proper 'notice' (although, depending on their manner or tone, such actions could be repudiatory and be the basis of a 'constructive' dismissal – see below – and could also be prejudicial to the fairness of any ultimate dismissal – see also below). This has implications for an employer's liability to provide pay in lieu of notice when the contract is later terminated.

'....notice that has been given can be cancelled'

The cancellation of notice is only legally possible if the party to whom the notice was given agrees to it being annulled. Otherwise, the notice stands and the termination will take effect.

Of course, there may be various practical or economic considerations that persuade the party receiving notice to agree quite readily to its cancellation. And there may be disadvantages imposed by legislation on someone who declines to stay in employment (for example, see the provisions on redundancy payments and suitable alternative employment in Chapter 11). But the contractual principle remains – agreement is essential.

Wrongful dismissal

Wrongful dismissal is a dismissal that is simply in breach of the terms of the contract (so, it is not a subject that is really covered by employment legislation).

Dismissal without any notice (summary dismissal) or without full notice is wrongful, unless the employee's conduct amounts to repudiation (for example, gross misconduct/negligence), or if the contract permits it (through a pay in lieu of notice, PILON, clause) as an alternative to working notice.

If the dismissal is 'wrongful', the employer can pay in lieu of all or part of the employee's notice entitlement (in effect, damages for breach of contract), but:

- the employer will be unable to enforce provisions restraining the ex-employee's post-termination activity; and
- the dismissal can still be 'unfair' under legislation (for this separate concept, see below).

The employee's remedy for wrongful dismissal is an action to recover financial loss (through an award of damages), either in the employment tribunal (maximum award £25,000) or the civil courts (no limit).

A dismissal with notice is not normally a breach of contract (but the dismissal can still be unfair – see below).

Written reasons for dismissal

A dismissed employee with two years' service can request a written statement of the reasons for dismissal to be supplied by the employer within 14 days of the request. This is admissible before an employment tribunal.

An employee dismissed while pregnant or after childbirth, so that her maternity leave period ends, must be provided with written reasons, regardless of her length of service and without request.

The employment tribunal will award two weeks' pay (no statutory maximum on a week's pay – see below – is applied here) for an unreasonable refusal to supply a statement, or if an inadequate statement is supplied, and may make a declaration of the true reason(s) for dismissal.

Unfair dismissal – the general regime

Qualification for protection

Unless a dismissal is found to be for an 'automatically unfair reason' (see below), an employee must have been 'continuously employed' for two years at the 'date of dismissal' in order to have protection.

Avoiding the service requirement for unfair dismissal: dos and don'ts

There are good reasons for giving all employees the same standard of treatment regardless of their length of service. And rushing to beat the two-year 'deadline' has its risks. Equally, however, there is little point in an employer allowing a situation to arise which will cost time and money unnecessarily. So, where applicable:

- make a date of termination fall at least one week before the second anniversary of commencement
- provided that the dismissal is not for gross misconduct, terminate immediately with pay in lieu of notice (rather than terminating with actual, working notice)
- phrase letters carefully. For example, make sure that the date of termination is not stated, or represented as, the date on which notice would have expired if it had been given
- ensure that no right of appeal against dismissal is described in a way that preserves, or might preserve, employment until the appeal is determined.

'Dismissal'

Dismissal occurs if:

- the employer terminates the contract, with or without notice; or
- a limited-term contract (one whose duration is set by reference to a period of time, the completion of a task or the occurrence or non-occurrence of an event) terminates without renewal; or
- the employer engages in conduct which is a significant breach or repudiation of the employment contract, giving the employee the right to resign without notice, and the employee, whether with or without notice, does resign in response ('constructive' dismissal).

To establish 'constructive' dismissal, does the employee have to resign without notice?

No. The vital thing is that the employee must, because of the employer's act or omission, have the right to resign without giving notice. If that condition is satisfied, the employee may, in principle, give full notice of resignation and remain working until the specified termination date.

Of course, in many situations of this type, that approach is not a practical one and not in the interests of either party.

Also, if an employee did give notice and remain at work through the period of notice, the (ex-) employer may well be able, in any subsequent tribunal proceedings, to draw inferences from the employee's behaviour. Is it an indication that the conduct stated to have caused the resignation did not occur? Or was it in fact not serious enough to give the employee the right to resign immediately and so to be the basis of a 'constructive' dismissal?

Frustration can be frustrating

A contract of employment can be 'frustrated' when an unforeseen event makes the performance of the contract impossible or very different from what had originally been intended. When frustration occurs, the contract ends automatically, without a dismissal. A prison sentence will not necessarily frustrate the contract. A significant factor is the length of the sentence. Where the contract provides for long-term sickness absence, a prison sentence of equivalent length may not be regarded as amounting to frustration. The difficulty is knowing when the point of frustration has been reached. If it has not, but the employer acts as if it has, a dismissal will result. And, it will often be unfair. So, generally, frustration is best left as a legal argument to be deployed in litigation.

Common misconception (4)

'...a constructive dismissal will always be unfair'

Not so. Strictly, establishing a 'constructive' dismissal does no more than confirm that there has been a dismissal – its fairness is a separate matter.

So, while almost all constructive dismissals based on interpersonal behaviour or attitude will end up as unfair, some derived from the breach of express contractual terms can be found to be fair.

For example, an imposed significant reduction of an employee's pay will be a breach of contract that entitles the employee to resign without notice. But, if the employer had a good business reason for the change and conducted appropriate consultation first, then the resultant constructive dismissal could well be fair.

Fairness of a dismissal

If an ex-employee complains of unfair dismissal, the employer must first show that there was, at the time of the decision to dismiss, a (principal) reason for it. To be admissible, that principal reason must be one of the following:

- capability, which can be about performance/skill, health, or qualifications
- misconduct
- redundancy
- continued employment in that capacity being illegal
- some other substantial reason justifying dismissal.

Then, the employment tribunal must decide whether, in view of the employer's size and administrative resources, the dismissal was reasonable in all the circumstances. This involves consideration of:

- *the quality of the pre-decision procedure* (including notification of, and formal dialogue with, the employee and sharing of information relevant to the situation). This is necessary unless the employer can safely conclude that the circumstances make such formalities 'utterly useless'
- *the factual situation or findings.* At the conclusion of the above procedure, were there, given the evidence available, at least reasonable grounds for continuing to consider the employee for dismissal?; and
- the ultimate choice *of the sanction or outcome of dismissal.* Were the factual situation or findings capable of justifying termination, even if some reasonable employers might not have dismissed? Were any reasonable alternatives to dismissal properly considered?

The 'band of reasonableness'

Different employers may adopt different approaches but each may nevertheless act fairly. In all cases 'there is a band of reasonableness within which one employer might reasonably take one view: another quite reasonably take a different view' (Lord Denning in British Leyland v Swift). If a dismissal falls within the band, and a proper procedure has been followed, the employer will have acted reasonably and the dismissal will be fair.

The tests for assessing whether an employer has acted reasonably in dismissing an employee were set out in *Iceland Frozen Foods Limited v Jones:*

- the starting point is the statutory provision that the employer must have acted reasonably in dismissing the employee
- in applying this statutory provision, the tribunal must consider the reasonableness of the employer's conduct, not simply whether they (the members of the tribunal) consider the dismissal to be fair
- in many (though not all) cases there is a band of reasonable responses to the employee's conduct within which one employer might reasonably take one view and another quite reasonably take a different view
- the function of the tribunal, as an industrial jury, is to determine whether in the particular circumstances of each case the decision to dismiss the employee fell within the band of reasonable responses which a reasonable employer might have adopted. If the dismissal falls within the band, the dismissal is fair: if the dismissal falls outside the band, it is unfair.

How will the tribunal assess the fairness of the reason for dismissal?

Depending on the reason for dismissal, the principal relevant factors that the employment tribunal will consider under 'reasonableness' are:

For Capability

- On grounds of performance/skill:
  - ➤ warnings
  - ➤ hearings/appeals
  - ➤ targets for improvement
  - ➤ assistance/training
  - ➤ alternative employment
  - ➤ being accompanied (at least, if the management of performance has a disciplinary aspect).
- On grounds of health (see also disability discrimination in Chapter 8):
  - ➤ consultation with the employee
  - ➤ medical report/information
  - ➤ reasonable adjustments (see also Chapter 8)/alternative employment
  - ➤ hearing/appeal.

For Conduct (disciplinary matters)

- quality of the investigation
- gravity of the situation (previous warnings or gross misconduct)
- notice of charges and provision of evidence to the employee
- Acas code of practice
- existence and handling of hearing and appeal (including being accompanied)
- the employee's previous disciplinary record
- precedents set in dealing with other employees.

Establishing misconduct

Employment tribunals apply a three-stage test in the case of most misconduct dismissals. The employer must show that:

- he believed the employee was guilty of misconduct
- he had in his mind reasonable grounds upon which to sustain that belief
- at the stage at which he formed that belief on those grounds, he had carried out as much investigation into the matter as was reasonable in the circumstances.

This test (the so-called *Burchell* test) arose from a case of dishonesty. But the principles laid down have become the established test for determining whether the reason for an employer's decision to dismiss was sufficient in all types of conduct case when the employer has no direct proof of the employee's misconduct, but only a strong suspicion.

For redundancy

- adequacy of consultation
- approach to selection
- consideration and availability of alternative employment.

In cases of redundancy, if selection from a group of employees is necessary, the selection criteria must be largely objective. That is, they should not simply reflect the personal opinion of the selector, but should be capable of at least some objective assessment and, preferably, supported by data such as attendance and performance records. Imprecise criteria that can be challenged, such as employees 'best suited for the needs of the business under the new operating conditions' and 'attitude to work', will be risky – unless they are then broken down and defined in more detail.

For illegality

Possible reasons include disqualification from driving, expiry or lack of a work permit, and breach of health and safety legislation. *(Note: there must be definite illegality involved, not just a reasonable belief in it.)*

■ discussion with the employee
■ consideration of alternative employment that would not be illegal
■ hearing/appeal.

For some other substantial reason

For example, the end of a limited-term contract, a change in the contract of employment or pressure to dismiss from a customer, regulatory body or another employee:

■ discussion/consultation with the employee
■ exploration of compromises or alternative opportunities for employment
■ hearing/appeal.

Dismissals of replacements

A person taken on as a temporary replacement for an employee on maternity leave, adoption leave or additional paternity leave (see Chapter 5) who is dismissed to make way for the employee's return will be regarded as having been dismissed for 'some other substantial reason' provided he or she was informed on engagement that the employment would terminate on the return of the other employee from leave. However, at least if the replacement has accrued the requisite continuous service (see above), the fairness of the dismissal is still subject to the test of 'reasonableness' (see above), particularly on alternative employment.

Dismissals connected with a TUPE transfer (see Chapter 9)

It is automatically unfair to dismiss an employee for the reason of a TUPE transfer itself.

However, if:

- a dismissal is for a reason 'connected with' a TUPE transfer, whether before or after it; and
- that reason is an economic, technical or organisational one entailing changes in the workforce (this requires a change in location amounting to 'redundancy' or a reduction in numbers or alterations to job content frequently equating to redundancy).

The dismissal will only be unfair if it is not handled reasonably.

Liability for a pre-transfer dismissal that does not satisfy these requirements and is, therefore, unfair will often pass to the new employer (the transferee).

Convicted offenders

It is normally unfair to dismiss for a 'spent' conviction (see Chapter 8), although the employee must have the requisite continuous service to bring a claim.

Unfair dismissal – exceptions to the normal requirement for service

The following reasons for dismissal are not subject to the normal requirement for a period of continuous employment.

It is automatically unfair to dismiss an employee:

- for being involved in proceedings to do with the enforcement of the National Minimum Wage (see Chapter 4)
- for refusing to work more than 48 hours a week or during a rest break (see Chapter 4)
- or signing a workforce agreement or opt out agreement; or for being an 'appropriate representative' or candidate in a workforce agreement on Working Time (see Chapter 4)

- for the following reasons, covered in Chapter 6, to do with a trade union:
  - being a member, or participating in the activities or using the services (at an appropriate time) of an independent trade union, or
  - not being a member of a trade union, or
  - being involved in the recognition or derecognition of a trade union, or
  - refusing an employer's offer of inducement
- for the following reasons to do with maternity (see Chapter 5):
  - pregnancy
  - giving birth
  - taking ordinary or additional maternity leave or receiving benefits during ordinary maternity leave
  - being subject to a requirement or recommendation to suspend work on grounds of health and safety
- for reasons to do with taking, or seeking to take, paternity leave, adoption leave, or paternity leave on adoption (see Chapter 5)
- for reasons to do with taking or seeking to take shared parental leave (see Chapter 5)
- for exercising, or seeking to exercise, the right to request flexible working, or for accompanying, or seeking to accompany, an employee who wishes to exercise this right (see Chapter 5)
- for the following reasons, covered in Chapter 5, to do with parental leave:
  - taking or seeking to take parental leave
  - declining to sign a workforce agreement on parental leave
  - being an appropriate representative or candidate in a workforce agreement on parental leave
- for seeking to take or taking time off to care for dependants (see Chapter 5)
- for exercising rights conferred on part-time workers (see Chapter 8)
- for exercising rights conferred on fixed-term employees (see Chapter 8)
- for exercising or seeking to exercise the right to be accompanied at a hearing, to have a meeting rescheduled, or to be accompanied by or to seek to accompany another worker (see Chapter 7)
- for exercising rights concerned with health and safety (see Chapter 7)
- who is an employee representative or candidate, for performing, or proposing to perform, relevant functions as such (see Chapter 7)
- who is a trustee of an occupational pension scheme, for performing, or proposing to perform, relevant functions or activities as such (see Chapter 7)
- who is a protected or opted-out shop worker or betting worker, for refusing or threatening to refuse to work on a Sunday or any shop worker for opting-out or proposing to do so (see Chapter 7)

- for being summoned or being absent to attend jury service (see also Chapter 7) unless:
  - ➤ the absence was likely to cause substantial injury to the employer's undertaking; and
  - ➤ being aware of that, the employee unreasonably failed to apply to be excused from jury service
- for making a protected disclosure ('whistle-blowing') in the public interest (see Chapter 7)
- for making a protected disclosure ('whistle-blowing') in the public interest (see Chapter 7)
- for asserting (to an employment tribunal or employer) an employment protection right available under legislation. It is irrelevant that the employee is not, in fact, qualified for that right or that the right has not been infringed, provided that the claim is made in good faith
- on grounds to do with a 'protected characteristic', because that is an unlawful act under separate rules (see Chapter 8)
- for taking, or having taken, part in official and lawful industrial action in certain circumstances (see Chapter 14).
- as a ZHW, for breaching an exclusivity clause in a ZHC or ZHA (see Chapter 2).

'Protected' conversations about possible agreed termination

Legislation allows an employer to initiate and hold discussions with an employee and to make offers to an employee about terminating employment on agreed terms (see settlement agreements in Chapter 13) which, if agreement is not ultimately reached, will not be admissible as evidence in any subsequent tribunal proceedings for general/ordinary unfair dismissal.

However, this statutory protection will not apply where claims about 'automatically unfair' dismissals (see above) or discrimination (see Chapter 8) are involved (a traditional, 'without prejudice' conversation does cover such claims, but first requires a dispute to exist between employer and employee).

Range and sequence of remedies

On a finding of unfair dismissal, an employment tribunal must consider reinstatement (same employment) and re-engagement (comparable or suitable employment) and must first ask whether the ex-employee wants one of these solutions. Practicability is relevant, but the engagement of a 'permanent' replacement does not make re-employment impracticable, unless this was the only sensible way of getting work done.

Unless it is not practicable for the employer to comply, punitive compensation (known as an 'additional award') can be awarded for the employer's refusal to comply with a reinstatement/re-engagement order. This compensation will be between 26 and 52 weeks' pay (maximum of £508 per week with effect from April 2018).

Also, in all cases, the tribunal will award standard unfair dismissal compensation.

Standard compensation for unfair dismissal

This normally takes the form of a two-part award:

Basic award

This is calculated in the same way as a statutory redundancy payment (see Chapter 11) and, therefore, has a maximum of £15,240 from April 2018. However:

■ From April 2018, £6,032 is the minimum basic award for dismissal for:
  ➤ non-membership of a union
  ➤ union membership or activities
  ➤ undertaking activities in connection with reducing risks to health and safety, having been designated by the employer to undertake such activities
  ➤ performing functions as a designated safety representative or member of a safety committee
  ➤ activities to do with being an 'employee representative' or 'pension trustee'
  ➤ a reason related to rights on working time.

Compensatory award

This seeks to look at the employee's true financial loss, including pensions and estimated future loss. However, in most cases, it is subject to a maximum of:

- 12 months' pay for the claimant; or, if lower
- the absolute 'cap' (from April 2018, £83,682).

The award is unlimited in dismissals for health and safety, public interest disclosure and 'protected characteristic' (see Chapter 8) reasons.

A tribunal may order a discretionary increase of up to 25% for the failure by an employer to follow the guidance set out in the Acas Code of Practice 1 on disciplinary and grievance procedures, although the cap on the compensatory award still applies for unfair dismissal.

A tribunal may also order a discretionary reduction of up to 25% for the failure by an employee to follow the Acas guidance. The limits on the awards are normally reviewed annually, for implementation from February.

The compensatory award can also be reduced by the tribunal if:

- the ex-employee has unreasonably failed to seek or take up work elsewhere (breach of the duty to mitigate loss) and/or has been guilty of conduct contributing to the dismissal (this also applies to the basic award); and/or
- the ex-employee could have been fairly dismissed for something discovered soon after dismissal (and before the tribunal hearing); and/or
- the tribunal believes the dismissal would still have occurred if required procedures had been observed and, in those circumstances, the dismissal would have been fair (often called a '*Polkey reduction*').

A reduction on any of these grounds is considered from the starting point of an employee's full, calculated loss before the statutory cap mentioned above is applied.

Interim relief

This is an order by the tribunal for the contract of employment to continue until a decision on the complaint of unfair dismissal has been reached. Ex-employees can apply for this relief if they claim they have been unfairly dismissed for:

- non-membership of a union
- union membership or activities
- 'whistle-blowing'
- undertaking activities in connection with reducing risks to health and safety, having been designated by the employer to undertake such activities
- performing functions as a designated safety representative or member of a safety committee
- 'employee representative' or 'pension trustee' reasons.

11. Redundancy payments

11   Redundancy payments

Scope of the right

The right is to a lump-sum compensation payment for an employee who fulfils the prescribed conditions and is:

- dismissed because of redundancy or
- laid-off, or kept on short time within the contract, for several weeks.

Conditions for eligibility

- The employee must have continuous service of at least two years.
- There must be a dismissal (unless the specific provisions on lay-off and short-time apply). For this purpose, 'dismissal' has the same definition as that used for unfair dismissal (see Chapter 10).

Dismissal for redundancy

Dismissal will be 'by reason of redundancy' if:

- the employer has ceased, or intends to cease, to carry on the business overall or in a particular place where the employee works or is based, or
- the employer's requirement for employees to do 'work of a particular kind' has ceased or diminished, or is expected to cease or diminish overall or in a particular place where the employee works or is based.

Possible disqualification from entitlement to a redundancy payment

An employee's entitlement to a redundancy payment is only maintained if the employee does not unreasonably refuse any offer of suitable alternative work that the employer makes before the contract for the redundant terminates. For this purpose:

- an offer on the same terms in the same place disqualifies the employee from payment
- an offer on different terms or in a different place raises questions of flexibility, suitability, and also the reasonableness of refusal (where the focus is on factors, such as travelling time and parental commitments that are specific to the individual).

There is provision for a trial period of at least four weeks in any new job that is offered. The expiry of the trial period is regarded as acceptance of the new job.

If, during the trial period, the employee terminates the employment for whatever reason, or the employer terminates it for a reason arising out of the change, then the employee is treated for redundancy payment purposes as dismissed from the original job. The employee therefore receives a redundancy payment, <u>unless</u> the new job was suitable and termination unreasonable. However, even then, the dismissal may still be unfair according to the considerations mentioned previously (see Chapter 10 and also below).

Common misconception (6)

'… the conditions governing entitlement to a statutory redundancy payment also apply to access to an additional "company" redundancy payment'

Formally, they do not. When an employment tribunal applies the rules in the redundancy legislation, its decision binds the parties on the statutory payment only. The entitlement to an enhanced payment, whether introduced in the contract of employment or in negotiation or consultation under a specific redundancy exercise, does not automatically follow.

That said, if there are no separate detailed rules in place, it will be difficult to resist practical and legal pressure to treat the additional payment component in the same way as the statutory. So, if it is intended to depart from the criteria used for the statutory scheme, it is sensible for an enhanced scheme explicitly to set down its own rules and conditions.

For example, it might provide that refusal of any offer of alternative employment (not just 'suitable' alternative employment) disqualifies an employee from the non-statutory payment.

Lay-off and short-time

An employee can claim a redundancy payment if laid off or on short time for four consecutive weeks, or for a broken series of six weeks in any 13 weeks. For this purpose:

- *lay-off* is no work and no pay of any kind from the employer for the week in question
- *short time* is shortage of work and less than half pay for that week.

Note: the statutory provisions on guarantee payments (see Chapter 4) use a different definition of lay-off, based on individual workless days.

The employee must initiate the process by giving the employer, within four weeks of the latest week of lay-off or short time, written notice of intention to claim a redundancy payment.

Entitlement then depends on whether the employer serves counter-notice within seven days, contesting the claim because there is a reasonable prospect of a sustained resumption of full working. If so, the employment tribunal decides. Payment, in any event, is made only when the employee finally resigns with notice.

The service requirement of two years applies.

This statutory right is only needed if the contract of employment allows the employer to lay the employee off and/or to implement short time. Without this right, the employee would be unable to claim a redundancy payment, regardless of the length of the lay-off or short time.

In contrast, if the contract does not contain lay-off/short-time provisions, an employee experiencing lay-off or short time can resign and assert 'constructive' dismissal by reason of redundancy in order to get a statutory payment (see earlier). The statutory lay-off/short-time rules are not needed.

Calculation of a statutory redundancy payment

The tariff

The calculation is based on a scale, working back from the date of dismissal:

- for each year of reckonable service from age 41   1½ weeks' pay
- for each year of reckonable service from age 22 to 40   1 week's pay
- for each year of reckonable service below age 22   ½ week's pay

A 'week's pay' is calculated according to defined rules.

Applicable limits:

- the maximum service taken into account is 20 years (a 'year' being 12 complete calendar months)
- so, if all these years fall at the age of 41 or older, there will be a maximum of 30 weeks' pay
- with effect from April 2018, the maximum 'one week's pay' is £508
- so the maximum overall payment is £14,670.

The maximum amount of 'one week's pay' (and therefore of a statutory redundancy payment) is reviewed each April.

'Indirect' age discrimination and redundancy payments

Although it is, in part, based on length of service, the statutory redundancy payment scheme is specifically exempted by legislation from any unlawfulness caused by 'indirect' age discrimination (see Chapter 8).

Any scheme for enhanced redundancy payments will also be completely exempt from such unlawfulness provided that it uses the statutory scheme's classification of ages and bases itself on the same sliding scale of 'weeks' pay' entitlement (see above: *Calculation of a redundancy payment*) before applying a common multiplier or ignoring the maximum on a week's pay.

Any other form of service-based enhanced scheme will need to satisfy the 'objective justification' test under age discrimination law (see Chapter 8).

Claims for redundancy payments

A claim for a redundancy payment must be made within six months of the termination of the contract (unless a claim for unfair dismissal is made within three months). The employment tribunal can hear a time-barred claim within a further six months, if that is just and equitable in the circumstances.

If the tribunal awards an ex-employee a statutory redundancy payment, it may also award compensation for any financial loss caused by the employer's non-payment.

Consultation on, and notification of, large-scale redundancies

There is a duty to consult representatives of employees (see Chapter 12).

At the same time as representatives are being consulted, there is also a duty to notify the Department for Business, Innovation and Skills (DBIS) on Form HR1 of the proposed number of redundancies. Failure to notify can result in criminal proceedings and a fine not exceeding £5,000 against the company and/or its officer.

Unfair dismissal and redundancy

A dismissal for redundancy may be unfair (see Chapter 10) on grounds that:

- the employer has failed to give the employee as much warning or opportunity for one-to-one consultation as is reasonably practicable (unless the employer can reasonably conclude, at the time, that such consultation would be futile), or
- the selection criteria used are unreasonable in themselves or have been applied unreasonably, or
- the employer has failed to consider and, if appropriate, offer the employee any alternative employment that was available.

Also, a redundancy dismissal will be unfair if the employee is selected for any of the 'automatically unfair' reasons referred to in Chapter 10. The normal service qualification for unfair dismissal does not apply to these automatically unfair reasons.

12. Consultation with employee representatives

12   Consultation with employee representatives

Basic obligation

An employer must consult 'appropriate representatives' of employees if it is proposing to dismiss as redundant 20 or more employees at one establishment within a period of 90 days or less.

Note: before a TUPE transfer (see Chapter 9) occurs, the transferee organisation, even though it is not yet the 'employer' of the affected employees, may, with the consent of the transferor organisation, consult representatives of those employees about redundancies it proposes to make once the TUPE transfer has happened.

'Establishment'

This is defined as the 'unit' to which the workers at risk of redundancy are 'assigned'.

One 'establishment' can be the amalgam of several workplaces at separate physical locations. Conversely, it is possible to have separate 'establishments' based at the same site. An establishment can sometimes be found to exist even where the affected workers do not have a specific, 'physical' workplace provided by the employer at all (for example, field sales representatives).

'Redundant' and 'proposing to dismiss' – who is counted?

The definition of 'redundant' is broader than that used for redundancy payment purposes. It covers any reason 'not related to the individual' – so it extends to proposed changes in terms and conditions and/or working arrangements that do not eliminate posts (reduce the staff) or alter the essential nature of jobs.

Whatever types of 'redundancy' are involved in an exercise, the question whether an employer is 'proposing to dismiss' employees has to be answered by reference to what might be necessary. For example, an employer might hope, often justifiably, that there will be sufficient volunteers to meet the targeted reduction or that employees will agree to changes in terms and conditions. But, if those hopes are not borne out, the desired results would require the termination of existing contracts of employment (a 'dismissal'). That possibility must be taken into account in counting the number of proposed dismissals.

However, employees on fixed-term or other limited-term contracts (see Chapters 3, 8 and 10), where the term is due to expire anyway during the period of the 'redundancy exercise', need not be counted as 'proposed dismissals'.

Employee representatives

'Appropriate representatives' are representatives of a recognised trade union or representatives elected by the employees.

If there is a recognised trade union for some or all categories of affected employees, the employer must consult only its representatives about those employees affected by the redundancy and who are covered by trade union recognition.

There is a loosely-prescribed method for electing employee representatives. This features the following requirements or standards:

- there should be sufficient representatives to reflect the interests of all the affected employees and of the groups within that number
- candidates for election must be affected employees
- no affected employee may be excluded from candidacy or from voting
- representatives can be elected to represent all affected employees or a particular group (the employer's choice)
- each voter should have as many votes as there are candidates, either overall or, if applicable, in the voter's designated group
- voting should generally be in secret.

Timescales

Consultation must begin 'in good time' and no less than 30 days or, for 100 or more proposed redundancies, no less than 45 days before the first redundancy dismissal is due to take effect.

Preliminary information that must be provided to the representatives

Initial written notification to appropriate representatives must provide information about the reasons for the proposed redundancies, the numbers and descriptions of the employees affected, the number of agency workers and the type of work they do, the proposed selection procedures, the proposed method of carrying out the dismissals, including the period over which they are to take effect, and the proposed method of calculating any non-statutory redundancy payments.

Scope of consultation

Consultation with representatives must be with a view to reaching agreement and must cover ways of:

■ avoiding dismissals
■ reducing the number of dismissals
■ reducing the effects of dismissals.

The first two subjects for consultation mean that it may also be necessary for the employer to consult about, or at least to explain or discuss, the business or organisational plan that has resulted in the proposal for redundancies.

Fair consultation about redundancy means consultation when the proposals are still at a formative stage. It 'involves giving the body consulted a fair and proper opportunity to understand fully the matters about which it is being consulted, and to express its views on those subjects, with the consulter thereafter considering those views properly and genuinely' (Lord Justice Glidewell in *R v British Coal Corporation & Secretary of State for Trade and Industry ex parte Price*).

The law requires an employer to terminate any contracts of employment or issue notices of dismissal only when the process of collective consultation has been completed. But this does not mean that a full 30 or, as the case may be, 45 days' consultation must have occurred. It is possible for the employer and representatives of the staff to agree that collective consultation has been completed before this or, without such consensus, for it to have run its course even though there is no agreement. The obligation is only to commence consultation at least 30 or 45 days beforehand.

Consequence of non-compliance

Failure to consult gives rise to a complaint to the employment tribunal and, if the employer is liable, to a 'protective award' of up to 90 days' pay (for this purpose, there is no statutory limit on the amount of a day's pay). If the successful complaint has been brought by the trade union or elected representatives (rather than by an individual affected employee denied their rights), this award will apply to each and every employee affected by the failure (whether yet made redundant or not).

The maximum award is the starting point for the tribunal: a lesser amount will only be awarded if there are mitigating circumstances surrounding the employer's non-compliance.

Basic duty and timing

The employer's obligations to consult arise before a 'relevant TUPE transfer' of a business or undertaking. For this and the effect of TUPE on individual contracts of employees in a business/undertaking, see Chapter 9.

The duty is initially to provide information, in writing, to appropriate representatives (see above) of 'affected employees' long enough before the transfer to allow any necessary consultation to occur.

'Affected employees' of the existing organisation (transferor) or the incoming organisation (transferee) are those who may be affected by the transfer or by measures taken in connection with the transfer.

Information to be provided

The required information is:

- reasons for the transfer and its approximate timing
- the legal, economic and social implications of the transfer
- the numbers of, and the types of work done by, any agency workers
- the measures envisaged by the employer or the fact that no measures are envisaged
- in the case of the transferor, the measures that it envisages the transferee will take with the transferred employees. Or, if it envisages that no measures will be taken, that fact. (To enable the transferor to comply with this, the transferee is under a duty to provide the relevant information to the transferor in good time.)

Possible duty to consult

The duty of those employers who do envisage taking any pre-transfer measures with their own employees is then to consult representatives with a view to reaching agreement on them.

No minimum timescale for commencing such consultation is set down, unless the measure is 'redundancy' and the numbers and timescales bring into play the need to consult representatives of employees about redundancies (see above).

If a transferee envisages taking measures after the transfer, TUPE itself imposes no duty on the transferee to consult before the transfer (because the transferee is not yet the employer).

However, if the measure is redundancies, the proposed number (possibly in any single establishment) is at least 20 and they will occur within 90 days or less, the transferee can undertake the separately required collective redundancy consultation with employee representatives (see above):

- after the transfer, once the transferee has become the employer; or
- before the transfer, provided the consent of the transferor has been obtained.

Consequence of non-compliance

Failure to inform or, if applicable, to consult gives rise to a complaint to the employment tribunal and possible compensation (of up to 13 weeks' pay, with no statutory cap) to each employee affected.

The transferee is jointly and severally liable with the transferor for other awards of compensation against the transferor arising from a failure to inform or consult.

However, if the transferor's breach arises from the transferee's failure to give the transferor information about the proposed measures, compensation is normally payable by the transferee.

Health and safety

There is an obligation on the employer to consult representatives of employees (or employees individually) on certain health and safety matters.

General workplace information and consultation

Scope and activation

The rules apply to undertakings with 50 or more employees in the UK.

The employer's obligation to consult arises only after a 'trigger' request. Should employees make a valid request, employers are under an obligation to establish means for information and consultation to give the employees a better idea of potential changes in their employment. To be valid, a request must be made in writing by 10% of the employees in the undertaking, subject to a minimum of 15 employees and a maximum of 2,500 employees.

Voluntary and pre-existing agreements

After the receipt of a request, and subject to the provisions about a pre-existing agreement (see below), the employer has six months (extendable by agreement) in which to negotiate a voluntary agreement with employee representatives.

If a voluntary agreement is reached, it must:

- set out the circumstances in which the employer will inform and consult the employees
- provide either for dealing with employee representatives or for the information and consultation to be directly with employees (or both)
- be recorded in writing and dated
- cover all of the employees in the undertaking
- be signed by the employer and approved by the employees.

The regulations provide for the possible retention of any pre-existing agreements endorsed by the workforce. A valid pre-existing agreement must:

- be in writing
- cover all the employees in the undertaking
- set out how the employer will inform and consult the employees
- be approved by the employees.

If the employer already has a pre-existing agreement in place when it receives a valid request, it may ballot the workforce to seek endorsement of the request. If, after a ballot, a minimum of 40% of the employees (constituting a majority of those who actually voted) endorses the request, the pre-existing agreement becomes invalid and negotiation on a voluntary agreement must commence. But, if less than 40% endorses the request, the pre-existing agreement will continue.

Standard, default provisions

If no voluntary agreement is reached by any required negotiation, 'standard' provisions will apply. This will require the establishment of an information and consultation committee, representing all employees in the undertaking, after the election of representatives. The number of representatives is proportional to the number of employees (one representative for every 50 employees up to a maximum of 25 representatives).

The standard provisions require the employer to inform and consult the employees and to provide:

- information on the recent and probable development of the undertaking's activities and economic situation
- information and consultation on the situation, structure and probable development of employment within the undertaking and on any anticipatory measures envisaged, particularly if there is a threat to employment within the undertaking
- information and consultation, with a view to reaching agreement, on decisions likely to lead to substantial changes in work organisation or in contractual relations between the employer and its employees. These include decisions entailing collective redundancies and business transfers – areas that are covered by separate obligations to consult employee representatives.

Subsequent requests from employees

If the employees have made a request, or negotiations have been initiated by the employer, no further request may be made for three years after the conclusion of a negotiated agreement or the application of the standard provisions.

Consequence of non-compliance

If an employer has failed to establish arrangements for information and consultation, an employee may complain to the Central Arbitration Committee (CAC). The CAC will deal with any disputes about the operation of such arrangements. Sanctions for employers involve a range of remedies based on orders to perform obligations under the legislation and financial penalties of up to £75,000, depending on the size of the employer and other factors. If the CAC upholds a complaint that bears a financial penalty against an employer, an employee may make an application to the Employment Appeal Tribunal for payment.

Pension matters

Scope of duty

The duty to consult on pensions applies to a 'relevant employer' with 50 or more employees.

A 'relevant employer' is one operating or participating in an occupational pension scheme (other than a small or public service scheme) or a personal pension scheme with the employer's contributions.

The duty to consult covers a 'listed change' to future arrangements under the applicable scheme.

Listed changes for occupational schemes

- raising the pension age
- closing the scheme to new members
- stopping future accruals
- ceasing the employer's contributions
- introducing or increasing the members' contributions
- reducing the employer's contributions (money purchase only)
- converting to money purchase (defined benefit only)
- changing the basis of future accrual (defined benefit only).

Listed changes for personal schemes:

- removing or reducing the employer's contributions
- increasing the members' contributions.

If the trustees or managers of a scheme instigate the listed change, they must notify the relevant employer(s) in writing.

Each employer must provide written information to those employees who are 'affected members' and any existing, appropriate representatives of such people.

The information for 'affected members' must include:

- a description of the change and its likely effects
- appropriate background information
- an indication of timescale.

Existing 'appropriate representatives' are those:

- of a recognised trade union
- elected or appointed under a negotiated voluntary agreement or 'standard' arrangement under information and consultation regulations
- elected or appointed under a pre-existing agreement for the purposes of the information and consultation regulations
- previously elected for purposes of occupational and personal pension scheme regulations.

The subsequent consultation by the employer must be with:

- one or more of the types of existing appropriate representative above and/ or (if a pre-existing or negotiated agreement under the information and consultation regulations provides for direct consultation with employees) with the affected members directly; or
- if existing representatives or direct consultation arrangements do not exist or do not cover some or all affected members:
  - ➤ representatives newly elected for the purposes of occupational and personal pension schemes regulations; or
  - ➤ if no such representatives are elected for some or all affected members, those affected members directly.

The consultation period

This must be at least 60 days. At its outset, an employer may specify the date for the end of consultation or for the submission of written responses.

If no responses are submitted by a specified end-date, the consultation is complete. If responses are received, the employer must consider them before deciding whether to make the proposed change. For this purpose, if the employer was not the initiator of the proposal for change, it must pass such responses to the initiator.

Enforcement

This is by a complaint to The Pensions Regulator, which can order the payment of a 'civil penalty' of up to £50,000 for a breach (but the regulator cannot order the reversal of the relevant change).

13. The Employment Tribunal – system and process

13 The Employment Tribunal: system and process

Composition

In full form, the employment tribunal has three members: the employment judge (a qualified lawyer) and two lay members, one with managerial or business experience and one with experience of representing employees.

However, on unfair dismissal claims and many other matters, the employment judge normally sits alone.

Representation

A party may choose not to be represented but to conduct its own case. If representation is desired, it need not be by a lawyer. Legal aid is not available (except in Scotland).

Steps before a hearing:

- 'Early conciliation' - a prospective claimant must contact Acas to allow it to explore a settlement of the dispute for a period of one month. Only if Acas certifies that this procedure has not resulted in a settlement will the individual be allowed to present a claim to the employment tribunal (with the Acas certification).
- The employee or ex-employee (claimant) completes the claim form (Form ET1) and lodges it, normally within three months (but capable of extension in certain circumstances, including the time taken by unsuccessful early conciliation – see above), with the tribunal.
- The tribunal serves a copy on the employer (respondent) and notifies Acas.
- The employer has 28 days to enter a response (Form ET3). If this time limit (or any extended limit agreed by the tribunal) is not complied with, the tribunal will normally issue a 'default judgment', finding in favour of the claimant.
- Acas assigns a conciliation officer to promote a settlement without the need for a hearing (see below).

Settling a claim

There are two legally valid ways of settling a claim (or a dispute over statutory rights that has not yet resulted in a claim) – a settlement drawn up after conciliation by Acas or a settlement (formerly 'compromise') agreement.

Conciliation

The process of conciliation is continued by Acas even where early conciliation (see above) did not succeed.

In conciliation, the Acas officer has no duty of confidentiality to the parties and cannot advise them on the merits of their cases.

Any settlement reached is recorded on a Form COT3 and signed by both parties or their authorised representatives. In addition to specifying the core agreement, the settlement will usually include a time limit for payment of any agreed sum and may feature obligations on other subjects, such as the provision of a reference and the maintenance of confidentiality.

Settlement agreement

This is reached directly, without the assistance of Acas, between the employer and the employee. The parties must be advised beforehand by a 'relevant independent adviser' (a qualified lawyer or, with certified competence, a trade union official or advice worker).

To be legally effective, a settlement agreement must be in writing, specify the claim(s) or proceedings it covers, identify the adviser (who must have appropriate insurance cover) and explicitly confirm that these conditions have been met.

Processing a claim

First, there is a 'sifting' stage, in which an employment judge reviews the claim (ET1) and response (ET3) and has the power to strike out either if it has no reasonable prospect of success.

There are various types of proceedings in the tribunal: a preliminary hearing; a full (or final) hearing; and a reconsideration.

A preliminary hearing can cover case management issues, preliminary/ jurisdictional points (see below) and/or the merits of the case. The tribunal may rule that a claim is inadmissible or, if it has no reasonable prospect of success but was not caught at the sifting stage (see above), strike it out. It may also require the claimant to pay a deposit to be allowed to continue with any claim, allegation or argument that is considered to have no reasonable prospect of success (maximum £1,000 for each such claim, allegation or argument).

The powers of the Employment Tribunal

Before the case is fully heard, the tribunal will specify one or more dates for a full hearing (frequently when first issuing the claim to the employer – see above) and, sometimes at a preliminary hearing (perhaps done by telephone), will usually direct either or both parties:

- to provide further particulars of the case
- to give relevant documents (or copies) to the other party, and/or
- to exchange written statements of the evidence of each witness who will appear at the full hearing.

Failure to comply with an order can result in the case being struck out and/ or the party being fined.

The tribunal can also order the attendance of a witness. Disobedience without excuse can result in the witness being fined.

Preliminary points

In order to give the tribunal jurisdiction to hear the case, the claimant may need to prove (if any of these matters is disputed) that he or she:

- is or was an employee of or worker for that employer
- is protected – not one of the excluded classes (such as Crown employees, police and mariners)
- is qualified to complain (that the time limit has not been exceeded)
- was dismissed – if applicable.

There is often a separate, preliminary hearing (see above) to consider one or more of these points, on which evidence from witnesses is permitted.

Similarly, a preliminary hearing might be necessary in a case under TUPE (see Chapter 9), to determine the preliminary (but fundamental) matter of whether there was a transfer and, therefore, who will be liable for any finding of unfair dismissal.

Postponements

A hearing may be postponed by order of the tribunal, either of its own motion or on application of a party for good reason.

A party is generally limited to two postponement requests. Any further request or application will be granted only where:

- both parties consent to postponement in the interest of exploring settlement;
- the request/application was necessitated by the act or omission of another party or the tribunal; or
- there are exceptional circumstances.

and, where the request/application is made less than seven days before a hearing date or at the hearing itself, with the possibility of a costs or preparation time order (see below) being made against the party applying.

Procedure at a hearing involving evidence

The party under the burden of proof starts by giving evidence through relevant witnesses (who take the oath or affirm) and supporting documentation. Any prepared written statement of evidence that has been disclosed in advance to the other party (in accordance with the tribunal's order – see above) is generally 'taken as read' (so that it does not actually have to be read out on the day). Each witness is open to cross-examination by the other side and to questioning by the tribunal. The same process applies when the other party in turn presents its case.

On completion of the evidence, each party makes a closing statement to the tribunal (the party under the burden of proof goes second).

The employment tribunal may give a decision on the day or later (a reserved decision). It may be unanimous or by a majority. It is always provided in writing, in either full/extended form (which is mandatory in discrimination cases) or in brief/summary form.

The remedy or award for a successful claimant can be considered at the conclusion of the final hearing (if the decision is given then) or at a separately scheduled hearing on that specific subject.

Interest, costs and penalties

Unless it is paid to the successful claimant within 14 days of the tribunal's decision on remedy, an award of compensation attracts interest from the day after the date of that decision. This is at the rate of 8% per annum.

An award for the costs incurred by a party in successfully bringing or defending a claim is not automatic. However, the employment tribunal has the discretion, and in a few specified circumstances the obligation, to make a costs order (in favour of legally represented parties) or a preparation time order (in favour of parties who are not so represented).

Where it considers there have been 'aggravating features' underlying a finding against an employer (such as deliberation, malice, the presence of a dedicated HR team, repeated breaches), and even if it makes no other financial award against that employer, an employment tribunal also has the power to impose a financial penalty. This is of 50% of the financial award (if any), subject to a minimum of £100 and a maximum of £5,000. Any such penalty will be discounted by 50% if it is paid within 21 days.

Enforcing payment by employers

If an employment tribunal's award (including any accrued interest) or costs order or any settlement sum is not paid in full after a period of 42 days or more from the date of the award, order or payment date specified under the agreement, the successful claimant may invoke a procedure to enforce payment.

An enforcement officer will issue to the offending employer a 'warning notice' containing a specified date, at least 28 days thereafter, by which the debt must be paid. If it is not, a 'penalty notice' will follow, stipulating the payment of an amount equivalent to 50% of the unpaid amount (minimum £100, maximum £5,000). If, within 14 days of the penalty notice, the employer both pays the unpaid amount (to the successful claimant) and the penalty (to the Secretary of State), the latter will be reduced by 50%.

Challenging a decision

Reconsideration hearing

The tribunal's reconsideration of its decision 'in the interests of justice' may be requested, within 14 days of the written record of the decision being issued, by a party to proceedings or ordered by the tribunal itself of its own motion because of:

- an administrative error
- the party's non-receipt of the notice of hearing
- the making of the decision despite the justified absence of the party
- the availability of new evidence
- 'the interests of justice'.

Appeals

These can be made, on points of law only, to the Employment Appeal Tribunal.

Subsequent appeals go upwards to the Court of Appeal (or, in Scotland, the Court of Session) and the Supreme Court.

Referral to the European Court of Justice

This may be possible for a ruling on the scope and interpretation of EU Directives and their effect on UK legislation.

Litigation in the 'ordinary' courts

These are the County Court, the High Court, the Court of Appeal and the Supreme Court. Employment disputes that are based exclusively on the contract of employment (as opposed to rights created by employment legislation) are sometimes heard by these courts as an alternative or sometimes as a practical necessity. For example, an employment tribunal can only hear claims for breach of contract if they are on termination of employment and can only award a maximum of £25,000. In addition, there is scope for an equal pay claim to be instigated in the ordinary courts (see Chapter 4).

14. Collective labour law

14   Collective labour law

Recognition of trade unions

What is it?

Recognition of a trade union is about the employer's acceptance of that union's right to participate in 'collective bargaining' on behalf of, and otherwise to represent the interests of, a category of workers.

Whether an employer chooses voluntarily to recognise it or not, a trade union can nonetheless seek statutory recognition for 'collective bargaining'.

What is 'collective bargaining'?

The scope of collective bargaining will often vary according to the way in which the right to undertake it has arisen in the first place.

If recognition has been voluntarily agreed;

Collective bargaining can, according to the particular agreement, cover any of the matters under the general statutory definition. These are:

- terms and conditions of employment
- physical conditions of work
- engagement or non-engagement of any worker
- termination or suspension of employment, or the duties, of any worker
- allocation of work or duties between workers or groups of workers
- disciplinary matters
- a worker's membership or non-membership of a trade union
- facilities for union officials
- the machinery for negotiation and consultation, and procedures on the topics above.

When statutory recognition (see below) is awarded

The scope of collective bargaining is then either dependent upon the agreement reached ('semi-voluntary') or, if the statutory default model is imposed, it is limited to a narrower statutory definition, which covers only:

■ pay
■ holidays
■ hours.

Legal status and effects of collective agreements

A collective agreement between employer(s) and recognised trade union(s) is not, itself, legally binding and enforceable between those parties. However, the incorporation of parts of a collective agreement into the individual employment contracts is the way in which a change agreed between employer and union becomes legally effective. The making of the new agreement on pay or another appropriate subject can vary the terms of employment, whether or not the employee is a member of the union. And, even if the employment contract does not have an express clause incorporating the results of collective bargaining, an employee in the bargaining group is generally treated as being covered by terms agreed between the employer and the union.

Legal significance of recognition

However it comes about, once the recognition of a trade union is established or acknowledged, it brings into being certain rights and responsibilities created by legislation. The major ones concern:

■ time off for officials, learning representatives and employees (see Chapter 6)
■ consultation on redundancy, measures in connection with a transfer of undertaking and, perhaps, pension changes (see Chapter 12)
■ the disclosure of information (see below).

Although these subjects might also be covered by aspects of an initial or subsequent 'procedural agreement' between employer and union, the relevant legislation applies automatically and cannot be excluded by the terms of an agreement or by the failure of an agreement to mention them.

There are other union-related rights that do not depend upon recognition. For example, protection against victimisation (see Chapter 6) and the right to be accompanied at disciplinary and grievance hearings (see Chapter 7).

'Compulsory' statutory recognition

Initiating the process

The statutory recognition procedure allows an independent trade union to seek recognition for collective bargaining on behalf of a specified group of workers. This group of workers is known as the 'bargaining unit'.

The union starts the process by making a written request to the employer for recognition. If voluntary agreement cannot be reached between the parties within a specified period, the union may apply to the Central Arbitration Committee (CAC) to decide on recognition.

What is the procedure if the parties cannot agree?

If the parties cannot agree, within a fixed period, on the appropriate bargaining unit for the debate on recognition, the CAC's first task will be to decide that question.

For an application to proceed, at least 10% of the proposed bargaining unit must be members of the union and, in the view of the CAC, a majority of the workers in the unit must be likely to favour recognition.

If the majority of the workers in the bargaining unit are members of the union, the CAC normally awards recognition without a ballot of the workforce. If a ballot is necessary, recognition must be supported by a majority of those who vote and by at least 40% of the workers who constitute the bargaining unit.

If recognition is granted, the parties must then seek to agree on a method of conducting collective bargaining. If the parties cannot reach agreement on this, they must adopt the CAC's procedure, which requires the employer to negotiate with the union at least on pay (excluding pension rights), hours and holidays. This enforced agreement will be legally binding between the parties.

Should either the employer or the union fail to comply with a bargaining procedure imposed by the CAC, the offended party can apply to a civil court for an order that the other party comply. Breach of such an order is a criminal offence.

What if the application for recognition fails?

Should the application to the CAC ultimately fail (after being allowed to proceed), no further application can be made by the union for the same or similar bargaining unit within the next three years.

Removing union recognition

There is a similar procedure, to be used in defined circumstances by an employer and/or workers, for derecognition of a union that enjoys 'compulsory' recognition.

What happens when TUPE applies?

Under TUPE (see Chapter 9), recognition, whether voluntary or statutory, will pass over to the new employer if the transferred entity remains distinct from the rest of the new employer's business.

However, although statutory recognition can only be cancelled using the prescribed procedure mentioned above, voluntary recognition can be ended immediately by the new employer if it wishes.

Disclosure of information

The employer must disclose certain information to recognised independent trades union(s) for collective bargaining. The union(s) must make, and co-ordinate, requests in writing and specify their relevance. There are limitations on the employer's obligations. The Acas Code of Practice *"Disclosure of Information to Trade Unions for Collective Bargaining Purposes' provides guidance on the disclosure of information. Failure to observe the Code does not itself render anyone liable to proceedings, but relevant provisions of the Code are taken into account in proceedings before the CAC.*

The sanction is a complaint to the CAC, which can make 'one-off' awards in individual contracts, based on what the settlement would have been had information been available to the trade union.

Union membership or recognition in commercial contracts

Any term in a commercial contract that specifies the use of only union or non-union labour is void. It is also unlawful to exclude a tender, or to fail to award a contract, or to terminate a contract, on grounds that anyone employed, or likely to be employed, on work connected with the contract is, or is not, a member of a union. The same conditions apply to contracts that specify recognition of and negotiation/consultation with unions or unions' officials.

Industrial action

The contractual consequences

Industrial action by workers, whether official (supported by one or more trade unions) or not, almost invariably involves, or causes, breaches of contract or other interference with contractual relations. Such breaches or interference may relate to:

- the contracts of employment of those taking the industrial action, and/or
- the contracts of employment of other workers, whether employed by the employer at the heart of the industrial dispute or another employer caught up in it, and/or
- commercial contracts of the employer at the heart of the dispute or those of another organisation.

What is the legal position of someone who organises industrial action?

Just as a breach of contract can itself be the subject of a common law legal action by the injured party, so can the civil wrong of inducing or encouraging that breach. In legal terms, that is what the organiser of industrial action (whether a union or an individual) does.

It is often more effective for an employer to seek legal redress from an organiser of industrial action, particularly a trade union, than from the individual workers who participate.

As a result of this, leaving the common law to operate by itself would mean that industrial action would almost always be unlawful and open to legal action, regardless of the circumstances. Legislation has therefore intervened to give organiser(s) of the industrial action protection from legal liability if it is 'in contemplation or furtherance of a trade dispute' and then satisfies additional requirements.

Trade dispute

A trade dispute exists when workers are in dispute with their own employer and the dispute is wholly or mainly about matters such as pay, conditions and jobs. This excludes disputes between union(s) and employer when none of that employer's employees is in dispute; disputes between unions or groups of workers; and, usually, disputes about matters overseas.

Additional requirements for statutory immunity of organiser(s) of industrial action

1 *Ballots.* A trade union loses immunity if its industrial action has not received majority support in a ballot of members employed within the group(s) that are likely to be called to take action in which at least 50% of those eligible to vote exercised their right to do so. Normally, if industrial action covers different places of work, separate ballots must be held for each one.

The ballot paper must summarise the dispute underlying the proposed action and indicate the period within which the action is expected to occur.

In certain parts of the public sector (non-ancillary work in health, schools, fire services, transport, border security, decommissioning of nuclear installations and management of radioactive waste and spent fuel), the majority support for industrial action must also constitute at least 40% of those entitled to vote in the ballot.

In all cases, the number actually voting includes those returning spoiled or otherwise invalid ballot papers.

The employer must have received at least seven days' notice of the union's intention to hold a ballot and must have had sight of the ballot paper (which must set out a summary of the dispute) at least three days in advance of the ballot. As soon as practicable after the ballot, the union must notify both all those entitled to vote and the employer of the result and provide the employer with information about voting patterns. Ballots with a potential constituency in excess of 50 must also have an independent scrutineer.

There is a supporting Code of Practice, '*Industrial Action Ballots and Notice to Employers*', which provides practical guidance.

2 *Notice and commencement of industrial action.* A trade union must also give the employer(s) subject to industrial action at least seven (if the employer agrees) or otherwise fourteen days' written notice of the start of that action. Failure to do so results in loss of immunity.

Industrial action must occur within six months (or a longer agreed period not exceeding nine months) of the date of the ballot. After the expiry of that period, any new or continuing industrial action will only have immunity if it is supported by a fresh ballot.

The supporting Code of Practice, referred to in 1 above, provides practical guidance.

3 *Secondary action*, such as 'blacking' and sympathetic strikes, has no immunity, unless it occurs in the course of picketing that is lawful under 6 below.

4 *A person who induces,* or threatens to induce, a breach of contract because the employer employs, or has employed, non-union members or fails, or has failed, to discriminate against them has no immunity.

5 *Pressure to impose membership or recognition of a union(s).* Unions or other persons who organise industrial action to put pressure on an employer to act in a way that is contrary to the provisions for union membership or recognition in commercial contracts (see above) have no immunity from legal action. Nor do those who organise or threaten industrial action that interferes with the supply of goods or services on grounds that:

■ work done in connection with the supply of goods or services has been or is likely to be done by non-union members, or
■ the supplier of the goods and services does not recognise or negotiate/ consult with unions or union officials.

6 *Picketing.* Lawful picketing is limited to:

- employees at or near their own place of work
- an official of a union accompanying a union member, whom he or she represents, at or near the member's place of work
- an unemployed person at a former place of work in furtherance of a dispute connected with dismissal, resignation or redundancy.

In addition, the following requirements must be observed:

- the union must appoint an official or other member familiar with the Code of Practice (see below) as picket supervisor (PS);
- the union or the PS must take reasonable steps to tell the police the PS's name and how to contact him/her;
- the PS must have a letter of authorisation, to be shown to the employer or its representatives on request;
- the PS must be in attendance at the picket (and outwardly identifiable in some way) or readily contactable and able to attend at short notice.

If it is induced by lawful picketing, secondary action will have immunity from liability – for example, if a delivery driver is persuaded to turn back, so inducing a breach of the driver's contract and of the commercial contract(s) for supply and delivery.

The supporting Code of Practice, 'Picketing', provides practical guidance.

Other aspects of industrial action

Liability of trade unions

Those who suffer, or stand to suffer, loss because of unlawful industrial action (action that does not meet the applicable requirements of 1 to 6 above) can seek a court order (injunction) requiring the union to restrain or delay the action and/or can sue the union for damages.

The union is responsible if its actions are authorised or endorsed by the executive committee, president, general secretary or any official (including a shop steward) or committee. If authorisation or endorsement is by an official or committee, the union can avoid liability if the action is repudiated by the principal executive committee, president or general secretary.

Limits on damages against unions

The upper limits on damages awarded against a union in a single set of legal proceedings for unlawful industrial action are:

if the union has fewer than 5,000 members	£10,000
5,000 - 24,999 members	£50,000
25,000 - 99,999 members	£125,000
100,000 or more members	£250,000

The dismissal of participants in industrial action

A <u>dismissal</u> will be <u>automatically unfair</u> if it is for taking, or having taken, part in official (authorised or endorsed by a trade union – see above) <u>industrial action that is also lawful</u> ('protected' by statutory immunities – see above) when the dismissal occurs in one of the following circumstances:

- during the 12-week, 'protected period' that starts with the first day on which the action was taken by the employee
- after the 12-week period, but when the employee's participation in the action stopped before the end of that period
- when the employee's action continued beyond the 12-week period, but the employer had not followed all reasonable procedural steps to resolve the dispute.

<u>Note:</u>
(1) *The fairness of a dismissal occurring during participation in official industrial action that is not lawful will not be considered by a tribunal unless some other participants were not dismissed at the time or (although all were originally dismissed at that time) some were re-engaged within a period of three months. However, those dismissed for having previously participated in such action retain the normal protection from unfair dismissal.*
(2) *Those dismissed at the time of their participation in 'unofficial' industrial action have no right to claim unfair dismissal. However, those dismissed for having previously participated in such action (which had ceased at the date of dismissal) retain the normal protection from unfair dismissal.*

Temporary replacement labour

Currently, there are restrictions on the supply of temporary labour to replace those participating in industrial action, although these are subject to Governmental scrutiny and may ultimately be abolished (see Chapter 2).

Collinson Grant

Watershed is the new brand for Collinson Grant's employment law services, distinct from its other consultancy services. Collinson Grant still helps firms all over Europe and worldwide to restructure, merge acquisitions, cut costs, boost performance and profit, and manage people. This builds long-term relationships. We have kept some clients for over thirty years.

Our emphasis is on results and value for money. We expect to give a first class return on the investment in us. So we do not recommend action unless we are sure that the outcome will be worth it. We are not afraid to give bad news, or to champion ideas that may not be welcome.

Skills – the sort of work we do

Our work usually focuses on organisation, process, people and costs. We use this simple framework to manage complex assignments – often with an international dimension – and to support managers on smaller, more focused projects. We help them to:

- restructure and integrate – following acquisitions or to improve profits
- rationalise the supply chain – we examine every process and interface to improve efficiency and service
- set up financial and managerial controls – we create robust systems to improve decision-making and reduce risks
- introduce lean manufacturing and refine business processes – we analyse and improve how work is done, and use new ways to create change and make it stick
- cut costs – we make systematic analyses of overheads, direct costs and the profitability of customers and products; this helps managers to understand complexity, and to take firm steps to reduce it
- manage people – we draw up pay schemes and put them into effect, guide managers on employee relations and employment law, get better performance from people, and manage redundancy.

Our staff are seasoned consultants who have held responsible executive line positions. We work in many different sectors for large private and public companies and also in the public sector.

Watershed - Professional advice on employment law

Employment law has always been an integral part of our work, now under Watershed. Our experience is that the right advice at the right time will avert problems or minimise any damage they might cause. Our support keeps costs down, allows busy managers to get on with their jobs and promotes better relations with employees.

Our core service to clients is built around

- advising managers on handling employee relations (often under an annual fixed-price contract)
- briefing managers on changes to employment legislation and on practical approaches to managing within the law
- drafting and revising contracts of employment, staff handbooks, policies and procedures
- preparing and negotiating severance agreements
- assisting with the legal aspects, communication and consultation arising from:
  - acquisitions and restructuring
  - large-scale closures
  - redundancy exercises
  - TUPE
- conducting employment tribunals.

Day-to-day business life should not be dominated by questions of employment law but the subject can rear its head in any facet of activity. Our role is to lessen the constraints of the law so that clients can improve their businesses efficiently. This applies whether we are dealing with a single employee or a major restructuring project.

Our employment lawyers and HR specialists have a wealth of knowledge and experience and provide advice and guidance that is pragmatic and commercial as well as technically sound. We are constructive business partners and our aim is to help clients save money.

We shall be delighted to tell you more about how we can help your business.

Telephone: +44 161 703 5611 or e-mail: info@watershedhr.com

Index

Change alerts (forthcoming changes in legislation) can be found on pages 10 and 14